LYON TRAVEL GU

Budget Travel Lyon That Will Blow Your Mind, The Weirdest Modern City Hidden Gems & Off-The-Beaten-Track Locations for Your Next Trip (2024- 2025 Complete Guide)

GEORGIA TUCKER

Georgia Tucker

<u>COPYRIGHT</u>

All Right Reserved©2024 Georgia Tucker

No part of this book may be reproduced in any written, electronic, recording, or photocopying without written permission of the publisher or author.

The exception would be in the case of brief quotations embodied in the critical articles or reviews and pages where permission is specifically granted by the publisher or author.

Although every precaution has been taken to verify the accuracy of the information contained herein, the author and publisher assume no responsibility for any errors or omissions. No liability is assumed for damages that may result from the use of the information contained within.

Disclaimer: The prices listed in this travel guide are accurate at the time of publication. However, please be aware that prices for services, accommodations, and attractions may fluctuate over time. Readers are advised to consider this factor and maintain an upward budget to accommodate any potential changes in pricing after the publication date. Travel costs can be influenced by various factors beyond our control, and we encourage readers to verify current prices and plan accordingly for an enjoyable and stress-free journey. Safe travels!

TABLE OF CONTENTS

TABLE OF CONTENTS..2

INTRODUCTION **4**

   10 REASONS TO VISIT LYON 6

CHAPTER ONE: PLANNING YOUR TRIP **10**

   PLANNING A TRIP IN LYON 10

   WHEN TO GO 11

   WHAT TO PACK FOR LYON? 17

   PRACTICAL INFORMATION ABOUT LYON 18

   LYON TRAVEL COSTS...23

   BACKPACKING LYON SUGGESTED BUDGETS 24

   USEFUL PHRASES FOR TRAVELING IN LYON.................25

CHAPTER TWO: TRANSPORTATION **36**

   GETTING HERE AND AROUND 36

   FINDING AFFORDABLE FLIGHTS TO LYON 40

CHAPTER THREE: ADVENTURE **42**

   BEST DAY TRIPS FROM LYON 42

   BEST OUTDOOR ADVENTURES IN AND AROUND LYON 52

CHAPTER FOUR: SIGHTSEEING **60**

   ICONIC BUILDINGS AND PLACES IN LYON 60

   BEST MUSEUMS AND ART GALLERIES IN LYON 84

   BEACHES NEAR LYON: WHERE TO GO FOR SUN, SAND, AND SURF
....97

CHAPTER FIVE: ACCOMMODATION **102**

Georgia Tucker

CHOOSING WHERE TO STAY IN LYON 102

BEST HOTELS IN LYON..121

CHAPTER SIX: SHOP LIKE A LOCAL 134

BEST MARKETS IN LYON...134

SHOPPING TIPS IN LYON...143

CHAPTER SEVEN: EAT LIKE A LOCAL 146

LOCAL FOODS YOU HAVE TO TRY IN LYON.......................146

BEST RESTAURANTS IN LYON...150

CHAPTER EIGHT 158

EXPLORING LYON'S BEST EXPERIENCES 158

LYON CUSTOMS AND ETIQUETTE 174

LYON ON A BUDGET 176

TRAVEL HACKS TO SAVE ON YOUR TRIP 176

THINGS TO DO IN LYON FOR FREE OR ON A SMALL BUDGET....182

CHAPTER NINE: SAFETY 188

A COMPREHENSIVE SAFETY GUIDE.................................188

COMMON CRIMES AND SCAMS TO BEWARE OF IN LYON 191

SAFEST NEIGHBORHOODS IN LYON 191

CHAPTER TEN: ITINERARY OPTIONS...................194

2 DAYS ITINERARY...194

A COMPLETE 1 DAY ITINERARY.......................................202

LYON'S TRAVEL APPS FOR YOUR CONVENIENCE 204

ESSENTIAL APPS FOR NEWCOMERS IN LYON 207

CONCLUSION...210

INTRODUCTION

Bienvenue à Lyon! As you hold the LYON TRAVEL GUIDE 2024 in your hands, you are about to embark on a journey into the heart of France's culinary capital, a city where history, gastronomy, and culture converge in a delightful symphony. Lyon, often hailed as the "Gastronomic Capital of France," beckons you to explore its cobblestone streets, savor its world-renowned cuisine, and immerse yourself in the rich tapestry of its heritage. This guide is your key to unlocking the treasures of Lyon, providing everything you need for an unforgettable adventure.

Lyon is a city that tantalizes the taste buds and captivates the senses. As you stroll through the vibrant markets, you'll encounter the fresh, seasonal produce that defines the city's culinary identity. From the traditional bouchon restaurants serving Lyonnais specialties to the innovative gastronomic scene pushing the boundaries of flavor, our guide will navigate you through the culinary wonders that make Lyon a haven for food enthusiasts.

Georgia Tucker

Beyond its culinary acclaim, Lyon boasts a wealth of cultural and historical treasures. Marvel at the UNESCO-listed Old Town (Vieux Lyon), where medieval and Renaissance architecture transports you back in time. Ascend Fourvière Hill for panoramic views of the city, and explore the traboules—hidden passageways that weave through the heart of Lyon. From the impressive Basilica of Notre-Dame de Fourvière to the vibrant Croix-Rousse district, Lyon's attractions are as diverse as they are captivating.

Our guide is not just a collection of tourist hotspots; it's a curated selection of insider tips that will elevate your Lyon experience. Discover lesser-known gems, navigate the city like a local, and learn the art of savoring a leisurely meal at a traditional bouchon. From navigating public transportation to embracing the city's cultural events, our insider tips ensure that Lyon reveals its authentic self to you.

Planning a trip to Lyon shouldn't be a daunting task, and our guide ensures it isn't. From practical information on transportation and accommodations to essential French phrases that will enhance your interactions, we've compiled everything you need to know for a seamless and enjoyable journey. Lyon's warmth extends beyond its kitchens, and our guide will help you navigate the city with ease and confidence.

Lyon is a city that invites you to indulge, explore, and savor every moment. The LYON TRAVEL GUIDE 2024 is your companion on this journey, designed to be as diverse and captivating as the city itself. Whether you're a culinary connoisseur, a history buff, or a seeker of cultural experiences, Lyon welcomes you with open arms. Are you ready to let Lyon's charm captivate you? Your adventure begins here.

10 REASONS TO VISIT LYON

Just a brief TGV journey away from Paris, Lyon provides visitors with a captivating glimpse into French life. As the nation's second-largest city, Lyon seamlessly blends the allure of an ancient capital with the vibrancy of a youthful and appealing metropolis. Here are the top 10 reasons why a visit to Lyon is a must.

1. The City's Architecture Is an Impressive Mix of Old and New

Despite its relatively modest size, Lyon boasts a wealth of historic structures, including renowned churches like Saint-Nizier, Saint-Jean, and the Notre-Dame de Fourvière Basilica. This historical charm converges with an outstanding post-modern aesthetic, symbolizing the city's rejuvenation. La Confluence, where Lyon's Saône and Rhône rivers converge, underwent a significant transformation from neglected land to Europe's most extensive renovation project. It now houses the remarkable Musée des Confluences by Coop Himmelblau, along with other intriguing edifices such as the Orange Cube and Euronews, both designed by Jakob + MacFarlane.

2. Lyon Has Quality Local Products

While Bordeaux is renowned for its wines and Normandy for its cheeses, Lyon, as the culinary capital, offers an unparalleled array of local producers. Despite challenges in the 2000s, Beaujolais has staged a remarkable comeback alongside the famed Côtes du Rhône, Mâcon, Burgundy, and Condrieu—all within an hour's drive. The city's markets and supermarkets prominently feature local cheeses and meats, showcasing the region's gastronomic specialties.

3. Visit the Cradle of Cinema

The Lumière brothers, pioneers of cinema, have left an indelible mark on Lyon's cultural landscape. This cinematic legacy resonates through the city's numerous theaters and the esteemed Institut Lumière. The institute provides a captivating exploration of the industry's origins and hosts the Lyon Film Festival in October in its own cinema.

4. Let Yourself Be Carried Away by The Roman Ruins!

Lyon's historical narrative as a Gallic cultural hub unfolds magnificently, notably at the Roman amphitheater of Fourvière. This architectural marvel, perched above the city, serves as an ideal locale for a picnic, inviting contemplation of the events that transpired over 2,000 years ago.

5. Discover the Secret Traboules in Lyon

A distinctive facet of Lyon's heritage, Traboules are concealed passageways threading through the city's buildings, originally used for silk transportation. With 500 Traboules still existing, many concealed in Vieux Lyon, the opportunity to uncover these secret passages adds a layer of intrigue to your exploration of the city. Simply push a door; you might unveil a hidden Traboule.

6. The City's Restaurants Serve Delicious Food

Contrary to expectations, Lyon boasts the highest density of restaurants per capita in France. Renowned globally for its gastronomic scene, the city is home to esteemed chefs, with the legendary Paul Bocuse, often referred to as the "pope" of French cuisine, standing out prominently. Lyon has consistently earned acclaim for the exceptional quality of its culinary ingredients and the esteemed reputation of its gastronomy.

7. Breathtaking Murals and Optical Illusions

Lyon's distinctive charm is further enhanced by a plethora of murals and visual delights adorning the urban landscape. From the Fresque des Canuts in Croix-Rousse to the Fresque des Lyonnais along the Saône River, these artistic expressions are but a glimpse into the city's rich tapestry. These captivating works are dispersed throughout Lyon, each deserving admiration for its unique aesthetic appeal.

8. An Outdoor Getaway

For those seeking respite from urban pursuits, Lyon offers a retreat into nature. A substantial portion of France's national parks resides in the Rhône-Alpes region around Lyon, complemented by various regional parks scattered across the area. Lyon's strategic location provides an ideal setting for year-round outdoor activities, including hiking, climbing, biking, canoeing, rafting, and, notably, skiing.

9. Festival of Lights

Each December, Lyon is aglow with the Festival of Lights, an illuminating spectacle orchestrated by renowned artists. Tracing its origins back to 1643 and dedicated to the Virgin Mary, this three to four-day festival captivates millions of spectators annually, transforming the city into a luminous masterpiece.

Georgia Tucker

10. The City's Various Museums Are All Worth a Visit

For those contemplating a visit to Lyon, be informed that the city hosts a myriad of captivating museums. Notable recommendations include:

The Museum of Fine Arts

The Museum of Fine Arts, showcasing works by Italian (Tintoretto, Veronese, Guido Reni) and French (Manet, Matisse, Gauguin) artists, as well as pieces by Van Gogh, Rubens, and Rembrandt.

The Museum of Confluences

The Museum of Confluences, an innovative institution delving into the history of humanity through interdisciplinary approaches encompassing scientific and humanistic facets.

The museum of contemporary art

The Museum of Contemporary Art, a dynamic venue for contemporary art enthusiasts, featuring rotating exhibitions within a structure designed by Renzo Piano.

We trust that Lyon's allure, encompassing its architecture, beauty, and gastronomy, has piqued your interest. We eagerly anticipate your visit, promising a discovery of the city's myriad surprises.

CHAPTER ONE: PLANNING YOUR TRIP

PLANNING A TRIP IN LYON

Arriving

A convenient means to reach Lyon is by train, with Eurostar services from central London via Lille or Paris taking under 6 hours. The high-speed TGV from Paris offers a swift 2-hour journey, making Lyon an excellent stopover en route to the Alps or the Riviera. One-way fares from Paris start at around 55€, with potential discounts available online at the SNCF website. Ensure your train is bound for Lyon Part-Dieu station in central Lyon rather than Lyon St-Exupéry TGV station on the city outskirts, as an additional 30-minute train ride is required to reach the center. Lyon serves as an ideal layover for those heading to the Alps or the Riviera.

Alternatively, a 1-hour flight from Paris to Lyon-Saint Exupéry airport, situated 25km (16 miles) east of the city, provides another travel option. The Rhônexpress tram link, running every 15 minutes, connects the airport to central Lyon (100m/328 ft. from TGV train station Lyon Part-Dieu) for 15.20€. Taxis, costing 50€ to 55€ during the day and 60€ to 70€ at night, offer a similar travel time.

For those driving, routes from Paris, Nice, Grenoble, or the French Alps are accessible, providing flexibility based on your point of origin.

Visitor Information: The primary Lyon tourist office is located on place Bellecour (tel. 04-72-77-69-69).

Georgia Tucker

WHEN TO GO

September and October are optimal months to visit Lyon when the city is less crowded with summertime tourists, offering cool autumn weather and vibrant foliage. Between November and April, the coldest and darkest months, present favorable opportunities for discounted airfare and accommodations. May also provides comfortable temperatures for visitors. However, peak tourist season occurs in June, July, and August. Music enthusiasts may consider planning a trip in June for France's Fête de la Musique, transforming Lyon's streets into performance spaces. Additionally, the Les Nuits de Fourvière festival in June and July combines music, theater, dance, and cinema in the Gallo-Roman theaters on Fourvière Hill and Parc de Parilly in the suburb of Bron. For jazz enthusiasts, the Jazz à Vienne festival at the beginning of July is a must, with Vienne's Jardin de Cybèle hosting free concerts during the event (tel. 04-74-78-87-87).

Lyon Weather Overview

Lyon experiences a temperate climate characterized by warm summers and cool winters. The city encounters rainfall consistently throughout the year, with the highest precipitation recorded in May and June. Here's a seasonal breakdown of Lyon's weather:

Spring (March – May): Mild spring temperatures in Lyon range from 6°C to 18°C. This season sees higher rainfall, particularly in April and May. However, the city adorns itself with vibrant flowers in parks and gardens, creating a delightful ambiance for visitors.

Summer (June – August): Lyon's summer is marked by hot and sunny weather, with temperatures averaging between 15°C and 28°C. This period constitutes the peak tourist season, leading to increased crowds and prices. The warm climate is perfect for exploring outdoor attractions like Parc de la Tête d'Or and Fourvière Hill.

Fall (September – November): Lyon experiences a mild fall, with temperatures ranging from 8°C to 20°C. This season witnesses reduced rainfall, making it a popular time for visitors. The autumn foliage in parks and along the River Saône adds a breathtaking touch to the city.

Winter (December – February): Lyon's winter is characterized by cold temperatures, averaging between 0°C and 8°C. While snowfall is infrequent, foggy and rainy conditions can prevail. The city's Christmas market and light festival in December attract many visitors during this time.

In essence, Lyon is an attractive destination year-round, each season contributing its distinct allure. Ensure to pack accordingly and stay updated with the weather forecast before embarking on your journey.

What You Need to Know

- **Lyon's Arrondissements:** Lyon is structured into numbered arrondissements or neighborhoods, with notable ones including Vieux Lyon (5th), Presqu'île (1st and 2nd), and Confluence (2nd).

- **Vibrant Nightlife:** Lyon boasts a thriving nightlife scene, featuring a variety of dance and music clubs, particularly in its emerging neighborhoods. Notable venues include Marche Gare and Le Sucre in Confluence.

- **Renaissance Heritage:** Lyon holds the distinction of containing Europe's largest Renaissance area, second only to Venice. A stroll through Vieux Lyon provides a tangible glimpse of this historical richness.

Georgia Tucker

What to Eat

Lyon hosts over 2,000 restaurants, with nearly 1,000 showcasing the local cuisine. Pork, or cochonaille, plays a prominent role, inviting travelers to savor charcuterie and try sausages like Rosette, Jésus de Lyon, and saucisson chaud. The salade Lyonnaise, featuring poached eggs, croutons, fried potatoes, and pork lardons, is a local specialty. Potatoes find various culinary expressions, from gratins to the paillasson Lyonnais, a grated potato and butter pancake.

Fine dining options abound, with establishments such as Café Sillon, Le Kitchen Café, and the Michelin-starred Auberge du Pont de Collonges and Auberge de L'Ile Barbe offering diverse experiences. Café culture thrives in Lyon, with recommendations like Jeannine et Suzanne and Kaova Café.

Exploring Les Halles de Lyon Paul Bocuse, a gourmet market, is a must for food enthusiasts. The market's stalls offer an array of delights, including cheeses like Saint-Marcellin, Saint-Felicien, and Rigotte de Condrieu goat cheese. The market's restaurants provide an opportunity for a delectable sit-down meal, featuring shellfish and white wine.

Entry & Exit Requirements

For travel to France, a passport valid for at least three months beyond the departure date (six months recommended) is required. Stays exceeding three months necessitate obtaining a tourist visa before arriving in France. Refer to the U.S. Department of State's website for detailed entry and exit requirements.

City Layout

Similar to Paris, Lyon is segmented into districts known as arrondissements, totaling 9 in all. Key tourist zones are outlined below.

Vieux Lyon, 5th district: This medieval quarter, characterized by narrow cobblestone streets and Renaissance traboules, earned UNESCO recognition in 1998. Once a slum, it has evolved into a trendy area for artisans and antiques dealers. Atop the old town sits Fourvière Hill, housing Roman ruins and offering panoramic vistas of the snow-covered Alps.

Place Bellecour, 2nd district: Lyon's premier square, Place Bellecour boasts 18th-century structures and a colossal Ferris wheel. To the north, designer boutiques and one of France's oldest shopping arcades, Passage de l'Argue, beckon exploration. Spend an afternoon perusing museums dedicated to silk production and ethnology.

Place des Terreaux, 1st district: Locals frequent bouchons, eateries serving traditional Lyonnaise cuisine, in this neighborhood. Noteworthy attractions include splendid Matisse paintings at the Musée des Beaux Arts and an ancient amphitheater within Lyon's oldest park, the Jardin des Plantes.

Fast Facts: Lyon

ATMs/Banks: ATMs are abundant, and Lyon hosts various branches of the international bank HSBC, including locations at 1 Place de la Bourse and 18 Place Bellecour.

Dentists: For English-speaking dental services, consider Dr. Alexandre Baroud at 74 Rue Pierre Corneille (tel. 04-78-60-36-68). Inquire at your hotel for additional recommendations.

Georgia Tucker

Doctors & Hospitals: Seek non-urgent medical attention from Dr. Dominique Faysse at 25 Rue Garibaldi (tel. 04-78-93-13-25). Families can contact Dr. François Payot at 51 Rue Waldeck Rousseau (tel. 04-78-24-85-09). The central number for most hospitals in Greater Lyon is: tel. 08-25-08-25-69, including Hôpital Edouard Herriot (5 Place d'Arsonval) and Hôpital de la Croix-Rousse (Centre Livet, 103 Grande Rue de la Croix-Rousse). More details are available at www.chu-lyon.fr.

Embassies & Consulates: The United States Embassy is located at 1 Quai Jules Courmont (tel. 01-43-12-48-60), open Monday to Friday from 9:30 am to 5:30 pm.

Internet Access: Allo Phone, situated at 12 Place Gabriel Péri (tel. 04-72-71-31-39).

Mail: A branch of La Poste is conveniently located near Place Bellecour at 10 Place Antonin Poncet.

Pharmacies: Grande Pharmacie Lyonnaise, found at 22 Rue de la République (tel. 04-72-56-44-00), operates from Monday to Saturday from 8 am to 11 pm and on Sundays from 7 am to 11 pm.

Lyon Money Saving Tips

Embarking on a journey to Lyon can be a costly endeavor, particularly during peak tourist seasons. However, with strategic planning and savvy financial insights, you can relish your Lyon adventure without straining your budget. Consider the following money-saving tips to make the most of your trip while keeping costs in check:

Leverage Public Transportation: Utilize Lyon's affordable and efficient public transportation system. Invest in a Lyon City Card for unlimited public transport access and discounted entry to museums and attractions.

Dine Locally: Opt for local brasseries and traditional Lyon restaurants (bouchons) to savor authentic and reasonably priced meals. Steer clear of tourist-centric areas where prices are often inflated.

Explore on Foot or Bike: Lyon is pedestrian-friendly and accommodates cyclists. Save on transportation costs by exploring the city on foot or renting a bike for a more economical sightseeing experience.

Strategic Discount Planning: Plan ahead and seek out discounts and promotions before your trip. Many attractions offer reduced admission rates for students, seniors, and group visits.

Off-Peak Visits: Avoid peak tourist seasons when accommodation and flight prices surge. Consider visiting during shoulder seasons for more budget-friendly options.

Opt for Budget Accommodations: Numerous hostels and budget hotels cater to travelers in Lyon. Choosing these accommodations can significantly reduce your lodging expenses.

Tap Water: Lyon's tap water is safe to drink. Save on costs by opting for tap water instead of purchasing bottled water.

Buy the Lyon City Card: Purchase a Lyon City Card for one, two, three, or four days to access 23 museums, unlimited public transport, guided tours, and various activities at an affordable bundled price.

Visit the free attractions: Discover cost-free attractions in Lyon, including wandering through Vieux Lyon, exploring Les Halles de

Georgia Tucker

Lyon Paul Bocuse, and enjoying the expansive urban Parc de la Tête d'or.

Picnic Pleasures: While exploring Les Halles de Lyon Paul Bocuse, create an affordable and delightful meal by picking up cured sausage, Lyonnaise cheese, and a baguette for a picnic experience.

By incorporating these Lyon money-saving tips into your travel plans, you can revel in the beauty of this city without exceeding your budget.

WHAT TO PACK FOR LYON?

When preparing your luggage for Lyon, it's crucial to consider the season and your planned activities. Here's a list of essential items to ensure a comfortable and enjoyable trip:

Comfortable Walking Shoes: Lyon is a city made for walking, so ensure you pack comfortable shoes. Choose footwear with good traction and support as you navigate cobblestone streets and hilly areas.

Layers: Lyon's weather can be unpredictable, so pack layers that can be easily added or removed based on the temperature. Include a light jacket or sweater, especially if your visit coincides with cooler months.

Umbrella: Lyon experiences frequent rain showers, making a compact umbrella a valuable addition to your packing list. Opt for one that is easy to carry with you.

Adapter: For travelers from outside Europe, an adapter is essential to charge your electronics. France uses Type C and Type E plugs, so ensure you bring the appropriate adapter.

Camera or Smartphone: Lyon's beauty offers numerous photo opportunities. Don't forget to pack your camera or smartphone to capture and cherish your memories.

Daypack: A small daypack proves handy for carrying essentials like water, snacks, and a map as you explore the city.

Toiletries and Medications: Pack necessary toiletries and medications, including sunscreen, insect repellent, and any prescription medications you may need.

Clothes For the Season: Tailor your clothing choices based on the season of your visit. Lyon can be hot in summer and cold and wet in winter.

By including these essentials in your packing list, you'll be well-prepared for your Lyon adventure without the need for unnecessary purchases. Wishing you a delightful journey!

PRACTICAL INFORMATION ABOUT LYON
Here's some useful information to enhance your Lyon experience:

Accommodation
Choose from a diverse range of options, including hotels, B&Bs, and campgrounds. Opting for accommodation near the city center is recommended, despite being slightly pricier. This choice saves time on transportation, allowing easy access to most attractions within walking distance. It's advisable to book in advance, especially on weekdays when finding available hotel rooms can be challenging.

Planning a successful visit to Lyon involves these practical considerations, ensuring a seamless and enjoyable experience.

Georgia Tucker

Acquire the Lyon City Card

Secure the Lyon City Card, akin to a city passport, granting you unrestricted access to public transportation and complimentary entry to 23 museums, including their temporary exhibitions. Additionally, enjoy complimentary river cruises, guided walking tours, visits, activities, and substantial discounts on premier leisure pursuits, shopping, and more!

What's Included:

- Complimentary access to all city public transport (bus, metro, tram, and funicular, excluding May 1), along with park-and-ride facilities.

- Entry to 23 museums, encompassing temporary exhibitions, and various discovery activities.

- Guided walking tour.

- River cruise.

- Discounts on numerous other shows and activities, including the Guignol puppet show.

- Self-guided tour.

Major Events in Lyon

Lyon, a dynamic city, hosts diverse events throughout the year. For music enthusiasts, a visit in June aligns with France's Fête de la Musique, transforming Lyon's streets into performance spaces for local bands around June 21. In June and July, the Les Nuits de Fourvière festival merges music, theater, dance, and cinema in the Gallo-Roman theaters on Fourvière Hill and in Parc de Parilly in the suburb of Bron. Prices vary based on the event and can be obtained by phone at [tel] 04-72-57-15-40 (www.nuitsdefourviere.com). Notably, for four days around December 8, the spectacular Fête des Lumières illuminates Lyon's churches, monuments, and neighborhoods.

La Fête des Lumières (Lyon Festival of Lights): Originating in the mid-19th century, Lyonnais tradition involves illuminating windows and balconies on December 8 to honor Holy Mary. In 1989, this customary practice became an official city event. Annually, the "Fête des Lumières" kickstarts the year-end festivities, attracting around 4 million spectators over four days around December 8. This visually stunning celebration is a must-see!

Georgia Tucker

Biennale de la Danse (Biennial Dance Show): Since September 1984, every two years, the city hosts the Biennale de la Danse. This festival unfolds across various venues, notably the "Maison de la Danse" (Dance Hall). Over two and a half weeks, the festival presents a vibrant array of up to fifteen different dance shows daily. Attendees can delight in parades, ballets, and diverse dance performances featuring both emerging and renowned artists.

Nuits de Fourvière (Fourvière Nights): An annual summer tradition since 1946, the Nuits de Fourvière festival spans two months and welcomes global artists to perform in the enchanting space of Fourvière's ancient theatre. The festival embraces various disciplines, including music, dance, and theatre. Over the past five years, it has gained immense popularity, attracting French and international stars like Vanessa Paradis, Julien Clerc, Juliette Gréco, Tracy Chapman, Iggy Pop, Sting, Bob Dylan, and Björk.

Biennale de l'Art Contemporain (Biennial Contemporary Art Show): Biennially, art enthusiasts can immerse themselves in the Biennale de l'Art Contemporain, featuring contemporary art exhibitions across multiple museums. La Sucrière, a former warehouse in the Confluence area, is a focal point. The 2011 edition showcased the work of 78 artists from around the world and drew more than 200,000 visitors.

Festival Lumière (Lumière Film Festival): Given Lyon's historical significance in cinema, it's fitting that the birthplace of the Lumière brothers hosts a major film festival. Established in 2009, the Lumière Film Festival celebrates cinematic achievements. Notably, Clint Eastwood was the inaugural recipient, honored for his entire body of work. Since then, illustrious figures like Gérard Depardieu, Jean Dujardin, and Ken Loache have graced the festival's spotlight in 2012.

How to Stay Safe in Lyon

When visiting any travel destination, prioritizing safety is crucial. Fortunately, Lyon is generally considered a safe city with minimal risks for tourists. Nonetheless, taking precautions can contribute to a trouble-free visit. Here are some recommendations to enhance your safety during your time in Lyon:

Be Aware of Your Surroundings: Just like in any city, staying aware of your surroundings is essential. Particularly when walking alone or in dimly lit areas, pay close attention to your environment.

Use Common Sense: Avoid exploring unfamiliar or poorly lit areas after dark, especially if you're alone. Minimize the public display of cash or valuables to reduce the risk of attracting unwanted attention.

Take Care When Using Public Transport: While Lyon's public transport system is generally safe and efficient, exercise caution. Keep a close eye on your belongings, especially in crowded spaces, and be vigilant against pickpocketing.

Stay Away from Demonstrations: Although protests in Lyon are typically peaceful, it's advisable to steer clear of such gatherings. If you find yourself near a demonstration, remain calm and promptly move away from the area.

Know The Emergency Numbers: It's crucial to know the emergency numbers in Lyon in case of unforeseen circumstances. The emergency number in France is 112, and the police can be contacted by dialing 17.

By adhering to these guidelines and maintaining vigilance throughout your travels in Lyon, you can ensure a secure and pleasant journey.

Georgia Tucker

Other Things to Know About Lyon

Additional Lyon Insights: For those planning a trip to Lyon, here are some pertinent facts:

- **Location:** Lyon is situated south of Paris in France, a member of the European Union.

- **Currency:** The Euro is the official currency. It's advisable to have some cash on hand, especially as smaller establishments may not accept credit cards.

- **Language:** French is the official language, though English is commonly spoken. Learning a few key French phrases can enhance your interaction.

- **Time Zone:** Lyon follows the Central European Time Zone, which is GMT+1.

Lyon, a charming and picturesque city, promises a memorable experience. Armed with essential facts and insights, visitors can optimize their trip and savor all that Lyon has to offer.

LYON TRAVEL COSTS

Lyon Travel Expenses: Similar to any travel destination, expenses in Lyon can accumulate swiftly. However, Lyon is recognized for its reasonable costs, ensuring an exploration of its offerings without straining your budget.

- **Accommodation:** Lyon provides diverse accommodation options catering to different budgets. Hostels start at approximately €20 per night, mid-range hotels range from €60-€120 per night, and more luxurious stays can cost around €200 or more per night.

- **Food and Beverages:** Lyon's culinary reputation may tempt overspending, but there are affordable dining options. Traditional Lyonnaise restaurants known as bouchons offer hearty meals at reasonable prices, averaging €20-€30 per meal. Street food, prevalent in outdoor markets and food trucks, is another budget-friendly choice. A pint of beer or a glass of wine typically costs between €5-€7.

- **Transportation:** Lyon's public transportation is cost-effective and dependable. A single trip on the metro, bus, or tram is €1.90, or you can opt for a 10-ticket pack for €16.90. For frequent users, the Lyon City Card provides unlimited public transportation and free or discounted entry to numerous attractions.

- **Activities:** Many of Lyon's prominent attractions, like the Basilica of Notre-Dame de Fourvière and the Roman Amphitheatre, offer free entry. Some attractions, such as the Musée des Beaux-Arts and the Lumière Institute, may have a modest admission fee, typically around €10-€15 per attraction.

BACKPACKING LYON SUGGESTED BUDGETS

Lyon serves as a captivating destination for budget-conscious backpackers seeking to relish the charm of France affordably. Here are suggested budgets for backpacking in Lyon:

Low Budget (Less than €50 per day): For travelers aiming to economize in Lyon, consider the following strategies. Choose budget-friendly accommodations such as hostels or budget hotels. Save on meals by opting for street food or utilizing hostel kitchen facilities. Explore cost-free attractions like Notre-Dame de Fourvière and the city's picturesque parks and gardens. Utilize the well-developed public transport system, favoring buses and trams over taxis for additional savings.

Mid-Range Budget (€50-100 per day): With a slightly more generous budget, enhance your Lyon experience with added comfort. Opt for a mid-range hotel or secure a private room in a hostel. Delight in meals at mid-range restaurants or treat yourself to Michelin-starred dining experiences. Explore paid attractions like the Musée des Beaux-Arts and the Musée Miniature et Cinéma. Enrich your understanding of Lyon's history and culture with guided city tours.

Luxury Budget (Over €100 per day): Indulge in opulence by choosing luxurious experiences in Lyon. Enjoy a stay at an upscale hotel or rent a private apartment for added exclusivity. Dine at Michelin-starred establishments and pamper yourself with spa treatments at the city's premier hotels. Elevate your exploration with private city tours or embark on a hot air balloon ride over the breathtaking Rhône-Alpes region.

Remember, your budget is shaped by your travel preferences. Regardless of your financial plan, Lyon offers avenues to economize without compromising the quality of your experience.

USEFUL PHRASES FOR TRAVELING IN LYON

Exploring France for the first time is a delightful experience. The extraordinary museums and monuments in Paris, the sunny Mediterranean shores, and the majestic mountains create unforgettable memories. However, not being familiar with French can pose challenges. That's why I'm sharing some useful French expressions to enhance your travel experience in France.

Encountering language barriers can be tricky while traveling, especially if you venture off the beaten path. Whether you aim to navigate Paris more confidently or communicate in smaller French towns, these everyday French phrases can prove invaluable.

17 ESSENTIAL FRENCH PHRASES FOR TRAVELING IN FRANCE

Whether you're on a week-long visit to Paris or planning an exciting road trip in the South of France, mastering these 17 essential French phrases is highly recommended.

PS: I'll attempt to provide a pronunciation guide for American-English speakers, as French and American-English pronunciations differ. For accurate pronunciation, I recommend using Google Translate.

1. Bonjour/Bonsoir - Essential Greetings

Bonjour (used before 5 pm) and bonsoir (after 5 pm) both mean "Hello." It's crucial to say these greetings in shops, markets, cafes, etc., to receive good service and avoid being perceived as rude. Saying "bonjour" is a sign of acknowledgment before making inquiries or placing orders. Pronunciations: "bon gour" for bonjour and "bon swar" for bonsoir.

2. Parlez-Vous Anglais? - Do You Speak English?

This phrase is vital to inquire if someone speaks English. While fluency in French may not be expected, making an effort is appreciated. It's considered rude to automatically switch to English without asking. Pronunciation: "parlay-vu ang-lay?"

Georgia Tucker

3. Oui/Ouais & Non - Yes, Yeah & No

Oui means "yes," ouais is a less formal way to say "yeah," and non means "no." Note that the "ou" is pronounced with a "wuh" sound. Pronunciations: "wee" for oui, "way" for ouais, and "no" for non.

4. Au revoir

"Au revoir" is the French way to say "goodbye." It's the phrase you use when leaving a shop or any other formal setting. Pronounced as "oh rev wah."

5. Bonne Journee/Bonne Soiree

These two phrases, "Bonne Journée" (have a good day) and "Bonne Soirée" (have a good evening), are polite ways to bid farewell. Use "Bonne Journée" before 5 pm and "Bonne Soirée" after. Pronounced as "bun gour-nay" and "bun swar-eh" respectively.

6. Merci

"Merci," pronounced as "mare-see," is a fundamental French word. You'll use it frequently, expressing gratitude when your food is served or when someone hands you something.

7. De rien

When someone says "merci," respond with "De rien," meaning "you're welcome." Pronounced as "du re-un" or quickly like "durian."

8. S'il Vous Plait

"S'il Vous Plait" translates to "please." Just like in childhood, politeness matters. If you want to order something, conclude with a "s'il vous plaît." Pronounced as "sil vu play."

9. Ou Sont Les Toilettes?

"Où Sont Les Toilettes?" is a highly useful phrase, especially when you need to find the restroom in a restaurant. Pronounced mostly as spelled, with "ou" pronounced like "ooh."

10. Pardon

"Pardon," pronounced as "par-donn," is a versatile phrase meaning "excuse me" or "sorry." It's polite to use it in crowded places like the metro when someone accidentally bumps into you or when you need to navigate around them.

11. Excuse-moi

This important French phrase, "excuse-moi," serves as a polite way to begin a request, such as asking for directions or getting someone's attention.

12. Je suis desole(e)

"Je suis désolé(e)" translates to "I am sorry" in English. It's a useful phrase, especially when you accidentally bump into someone, make a mistake, or need to apologize. Pronounced as "ge swee dezo-lay," with the additional "e" for the feminine version.

Georgia Tucker

13. Je voudrais

For beginners ordering at a café or restaurant, "Je voudrais" means "I would like..." Pronounced as "ge voo-dray," it is a polite way to express your order, like asking for a croissant: "Bonjour, je voudrais un croissant, s'il vous plaît."

14. Je vais prendre

Similar to "je voudrais," "Je vais prendre" is commonly used when ordering food or drinks. It means "I will take" and is pronounced as "ge vay prend-ruh." For example, ordering a croissant: "Bonjour, je vais prendre un croissant, s'il vous plaît."

15. Je ne comprend pas

"Je ne comprends pas" is a crucial phrase when someone speaks too fast or when you simply don't understand. Pronounced as "ge nuh com-prond pas," you can also say "Je comprends pas."

17. Je ne parle pas le francais

"Je ne parle pas le français" is handy when someone starts speaking French to you, and you don't understand. Pronounced mostly as it reads, with the "je" pronounced as the same "ge" sound as "bonjour." You can also say "Je parle pas le français," which means the same thing. These phrases are essential for travel in France.

Want to Learn More French? Here are some great resources!

Are you interested in expanding your knowledge of French? Suppose you've already mastered the essential French phrases and are eager to enhance your skills. Whether you're planning an extended stay in

France or simply aiming to go beyond the basics, there are numerous resources available.

Learning Platforms

Numerous options, such as language learning apps like Duolingo and Babbel, provide effective ways to study French. Consider enrolling in online courses, such as those offered on the Comme Une Francaise website. These classes not only cover the fundamentals but also delve into advanced topics like conversational French for a more fluent speaking experience.

Educational Materials

Explore a variety of educational materials, including books like "Easy French Step-by-Step" and online platforms like Comme Une Francaise's paid classes. These resources offer a comprehensive learning experience, aiding you in mastering both the basics and more nuanced aspects of the language.

French Television for Language Learning

As you progress in your French studies, consider watching popular French Netflix shows like Lupin, The Ultimatum: France, Call My Agent, The Hookup Plan, and The Circle France. These shows provide an excellent opportunity to familiarize yourself with authentic French pronunciation and accent, contributing to improved language skills. Additionally, they offer insights into French culture, particularly in reality shows like The Ultimatum: France and The Circle France.

Phrases for Eating Out in Restaurants

When dining in French cities, waiters may have some knowledge of English. However, making an effort to greet them and place orders in French is appreciated. In smaller villages where English proficiency is less common, having essential French phrases at your disposal is crucial. You can print or store them in a notes app. Some useful phrases include:

- Waiter - Monsieur/Madame - / m'syhur / mah-dam / (Do not say "garçon." It's considered a bit of an insult)

- I'll have - Je prendrai - / zhe prawn-dray /

- Do you have...? Avez-vous...? - / ah-vay voo /

- The check - L'addition - / lah-di-shyon /

- A cup - Une tasse - / oon tahs /

- A glass - Un verre - / uhn vehr /

- A fork - Une fourchette - / oon foor-shet /

- A spoon - Une cuillère - / oon kuy-ehr /

- A knife - Un couteau - / uhn koo-toh /

- Some salt / pepper - Du sel/poivre - / dew sehl/pwahv /

- Appetizers - Les entrées - / lays-on-tray /

- Main courses - Les plats - / lay plah /

- Desserts - Les desserts - / lay day-ser /

Phrases And Vocabulary for Shopping in France

In French stores, it's customary for sales assistants not to approach customers actively. This is because they believe it's better to allow you to browse at your pace without interruption. They trust that you'll seek assistance when needed. When approaching a sales assistant, it's advisable to greet them first with "Bonjour Madame!" or "Excusez-moi Monsieur...?" and perhaps "Parlez-vous anglais?" before expressing your needs. This polite introduction can break the ice and make them more inclined to assist you.

Georgia Tucker

Shopping Vocabulary:

- Open - Ouvert - / oo-vehr /

- Closed - Fermé - / fair-may /

- I would like... - Je voudrais... - / Zhe voo-dray /

- How much is it? - Combien ça coûte? - / Cohm-by-en sah coot /

- May I try it on? - Puis-je l'essayer - / Pwee zhe leh-say-ay /

- I'll take it - Je le prendrai - / Zhe le prawn-dray /

- Store - Le magasin - / le mah-gah-zahn /

- A dress - La robe - / la rob /

- A skirt - La jupe - / la zjoop /

- A shirt - La chemise - / la shem-eez /

- Pants - Les pantalons - / pahn-ta-lon /

- Shoes - Chaussures - / show-seh /

- Socks - Chaussettes - / show-set /

16. L'addition s'il vous plait

In France, servers don't frequently check on tables, so if you need to pay, flag them down politely. Avoid snapping fingers and yelling "garçon." Instead, make eye contact, give a small wave, and say "L'addition s'il vous plaît" meaning "The bill, please." Pronounced as it looks, "L'addition," and "s'il vous plaît" as "sil vu play."

Getting Around and Asking for Directions

When approaching unfamiliar individuals, it's polite to begin with "Excusez-moi Madame/Monsieur," followed by "parlez-vous anglais?" or another question if you feel confident.

- Where? - Où? - / Oo ? /

- Where is...? - Où se trouve? Où est... ? - / oo-ce-troove / oo eh /

- Where is the train station? - Où est la gare? - / oo eh la gahr? /

- Where are the toilets? - Où sont les toilettes? - / oo son les twa-let? /

Essential French Phrases

Now that you've gained some insights into French pronunciation, it's time to put your skills into practice. Even if you only learn a few things in French, it's essential to master these key expressions. We've provided the phonetic pronunciation to assist you in understanding how they sound. Additionally, we've compiled a list of apps that can further aid you in perfecting your pronunciation.

- Hello - Bonjour - / bohn-zhoor /

- Goodbye - Au revoir - / oh-rev-vwha /

- Excuse me - Excusez-moi - / ex-koo-say mwa /

- I don't speak French - Je ne parle pas français - / Zhe ne parl pah frahn-say /

- Do you speak English? - Parlez-vous anglais? - / par-lay voo ahn-glay /

- I don't understand - Je ne comprends pas - / Zhe ne cohmp-ron pas /

Georgia Tucker

- Please - S'il vous plaît - / seel-voo-play /

- Thank you - Merci - / mare-see /

- Yes - Oui - / we /

- No - Non – / noh /

- My name is... - Je m'appelle... - / Zhe mah-pel /

- You're welcome - Pas de quoi - / Pah-de-kwah /

Additional Useful Phrases and Seeking Clarification
If you find it challenging to understand someone, consider asking them to slow down or write down information.

- Could you speak more slowly, please? - Pourriez-vous parler plus lentement? - / puri-ay voo par-lay plu lontamon? /

- Could you repeat that, please? - Pourriez-vous répéter, s'il vous plaît ? - / puri-ay voo reh-peh-tay, seel voo play? /

- Could you write that down for me, please? Pourriez-vous l'écrire, s'il vous plaît? - / puri-ay voo leh-creer, seel voo play? /

CHAPTER TWO: TRANSPORTATION

GETTING HERE AND AROUND

Getting Around Lyon

Optimal mobility in Lyon involves a strategic blend of walking and utilizing the city's public transportation system. The complexities associated with driving, particularly during the bustling summer season with traffic congestion and parking challenges, make it a less favorable option. Taxis and the Uber ride-hailing app are available, albeit as relatively pricier alternatives.

Lyon–Saint-Exupéry Airport (LYS) serves as the primary international gateway for most travelers. Commuting the approximately 20 miles from the airport to the city can be accomplished through various means. A tram station links the airport to Gare de Lyon-Part-Dieu, the main train station, while taxis are abundant, with fares ranging from 50 to 70 euros ($60 to $84), contingent on the time of day. Uber services are also operational. Rental cars, both at the airport and within the city, offer additional transportation choices.

For those arriving via high-speed trains from neighboring cities like Paris, Marseille, Nice, or Brussels, the TGV-operated train presents a convenient mode for day trips to and from these destinations.

On Foot or By Bike

While exploring Lyon's distinct neighborhoods on foot is encouraged, the city's expansive layout necessitates additional means of transportation. Biking, particularly along the scenic riverfront, provides a delightful alternative. Numerous bike rental

Georgia Tucker

shops and the city's bike-share program, Vélo'v, with a nominal daily fee of 1.50 euros (less than $2), facilitate easy access to bicycles.

Car and Car Rental

Although a rental car proves advantageous for ventures beyond Lyon, it is dispensable for intra-city exploration. Negotiating unfamiliar streets and securing parking can be challenging in a new urban environment. While an international driving permit is not mandatory for stays under 90 days in France, it is advisable. However, for excursions to the wine regions surrounding the city, rental services such as Avis, Hertz, Europcar, Sixt, and Budget are available at Lyon Part Dieu train station. Navigating the narrow streets of the old town is best achieved on foot, while accessing Fourvière Hill is most convenient via the Funicular Railway.

Public Transport

Lyon's comprehensive transportation network, managed by Transports en commun lyonnais (TCL), encompasses over 130 bus lines, five tram lines, four metro lines, and two funicular lines. Operating generally from 5 a.m. to midnight, each mode of transport requires a ticket priced at 1.90 euros (about $2.20) for one hour of travel across the TCL network. Alternatively, a 24-hour ticket is available for 5.80 euros (around $7). These transportation costs are integrated into the Lyon City Card, which also includes access to various attractions and activities. Tickets can be conveniently obtained from vending machines at subway and tram stations, as well as at kiosks displaying the TCL logo.

- TCL

- Lyon City Card

Taxi

Renting and parking a car can be a costly and time-consuming endeavor, especially when Lyon boasts one of the most efficient taxi services. Contact Taxi Radio de Lyon at www.taxilyon.com or call 04-72-10-86-86, and witness the prompt arrival of a taxi at your doorstep. Taxis are readily available throughout the city, with concentrations at train stations, Rue de la Barre near Place Bellecour, the northern end of Rue Édouard-Herriot in the 1st arrondissement, and Quai Romain Rolland in Vieux Lyon. Recommended companies include Allo Taxis, Taxis Lyonnais, and the presence of Uber adds to the convenience.

- Allo Taxis

- Taxis Lyonnais

- Uber

Tram

Inspired by the historical Croix-Rousse funicular, the Lyon city tram offers a captivating 1-hour tour through La Croix Rousse district (€10 for adults, €6 for children aged 4–11). Winding through narrow streets, the tram provides scenic views of the Gallo-Roman amphitheater, with stops at the silk workshop and traboules. Operating from 5 am to midnight, trams run every 5 to 15 minutes based on the line. For more details, visit www.lyoncitytour.fr.

Métro

Lyon's comprehensive transportation network includes Métro lines, trams, and buses. Obtain a pocket map (plan de poche) at any TCL office (www.tcl.fr; tel. 04-26-10-12-12), which oversees all mass transit. Tickets, priced at 2€ per ride or 19€ for a carnet of 10 tickets, are valid across all public transport modes. Purchase tickets from tram drivers or machines at metro stations (note that machines may not accept certain notes or international credit cards). For short-term visitors, consider a 24-hour pass for €6.50, a 48-hour pass for €12.50, or a 72-hour pass for €17.

Getting to Lyon: A Convenient Guide

Arriving in Lyon is a straightforward process, regardless of your starting point.

By Car: If you're already in France, driving to Lyon is a viable option. From Northern France, the A6 Motorway provides a direct route from Paris in approximately four and a half hours. For those in Southern France, the A7 Motorway connects Lyon to Marseille or Montpellier in about three hours.

Opting for the Train? For convenient travel from anywhere in France, consider taking the TGV. The journey takes approximately one and a half hours from Marseille, two hours from Paris or Montpellier, three hours from Lille, and less than four hours from Strasbourg or Toulouse. It might also be a cost-effective alternative to driving.

Fly to Lyon! For international travelers, flying is a viable option. Lyon Saint-Exupéry Airport is well-connected to almost every European city with direct flights operated by various airlines such as Air France, British Airways, Lufthansa, and Emirates. Travelers from Australia and America can reach Lyon through connecting flights from major hubs like Paris-Charles-De-Gaulle, London-Heathrow, or Frankfurt.

FINDING AFFORDABLE FLIGHTS TO LYON

Lyon is an ideal choice for travelers on a budget, but securing reasonably priced flights can present a challenge. To assist you in finding the best flight deals to Lyon, consider the following tips:

Utilize Flight Search Engines: Simplify your search by using flight search engines like Kayak, Skyscanner, or Google Flights. These platforms compare prices across various airlines and travel agencies, facilitating the discovery of the most economical flights.

Flexibility with Travel Dates: Enhance your chances of savings by being flexible with your travel dates. Avoiding peak tourist seasons, when prices are typically higher, can contribute to more budget-friendly flight options.

Advance Flight Booking: Save on costs by booking your Lyon flight well in advance. Aim to secure your flight at least three months before your departure date, as prices tend to rise as the travel date approaches.

Midweek Travel: Opting for midweek flights, particularly on Tuesdays and Wednesdays, can lead to more affordable options. Steering clear of weekend flights, which often incur higher costs due to increased demand, is a strategy to consider for Lyon-bound savings.

Explore Budget Airlines: Numerous budget airlines, such as Ryanair and EasyJet, offer economical flights to Lyon from major European cities. Keep an eye on sales and discounts, factoring in additional fees for baggage and seat selection when making price comparisons.

By incorporating these strategies, you can uncover cost-effective flight options to Lyon, contributing to overall savings on your travel expenses. Wishing you pleasant and budget-friendly travels!

Georgia Tucker

CHAPTER THREE: ADVENTURE

BEST DAY TRIPS FROM LYON

Are you in search of remarkable day trips from Lyon, France? Look no further – read on! If you find yourself planning a last-minute trip to or from Lyon, we have you covered with top-notch tours, hotels, and more! Here are some of the best day trips you can embark on:

Best Day Trips From Lyon

1. Beaujolais Wine Trail
Distance from Lyon: 49.1 km (52 minutes)

The Beaujolais Wine Trail, a 140km circuit from Chânes to Lyon, is a splendid continuation of the Burgundy Wine Route. A must-do in Lyon, it showcases valleys, hills, and the 10 signature crus of areas like Saint-Amour and Moulin-à-Vent. Highlights include Argigny Castle and the Mont Brouilly chapel, leading to the Pierres Dorées country. The 39 ochre-colored stone villages, resembling "Little

Tuscany," boast old churches and castles, with Marcy, Charnay, and Oingt being among the must-visit villages.

Getting there: As public transport isn't ideal for exploring wine regions, an organized wine tour is recommended for the best experience.

2. Dijon

Distance from Lyon: 197 km (2 hours, 9 minutes)

Dijon, renowned for its mustard, is a gastronomic haven in France. Explore its culinary delights at Les Halles and relish affordable tasting menus at Michelin-starred gems like Parapluie and L'Essentiel. Discover local cuisine at Mulot et Petitjean, a spice-based bread factory and museum. Visit the iconic Église Notre-Dame, the Palace of the Dukes of Burgundy, and stroll Rue Musette.

Getting there: Travel to Dijon from Lyon conveniently with regular trains completing the journey in 2 hours.

3. Annecy
Distance from Lyon: 145.6 km (1 hour, 43 minutes)

Overview: Immerse yourself in the charm of Annecy, located just under 150 km from Lyon. Known for the cleanest lake in Europe and its fairy tale-like village, Annecy offers enchanting attractions in the Vieille Ville. The lakefront showcases the Jardins de l'Europe, charming creperies, and glaciers. Explore the medieval stone structure, Palais de l'Isle, housing a museum of local architecture. A stroll around the lake, boat rentals, and visits to Musée-Château d'Annecy add to the experience. Indulge in shopping and dining on the picturesque Rue Sainte-Claire.

Getting there: Conveniently reach Annecy from Lyon with regular buses and trains, with the fastest connections taking approximately 2 hours. Consider the price as a deciding factor, as buses generally offer a more economical option.

4. Domaine de Lacroix-Laval
Distance from Lyon: 14.1 km (23 minutes)

Overview: Located northwest of Lyon, Domaine de Lacroix-Laval is a sprawling 115-hectare landscaped park, the largest of its kind in the region. Encompassing diverse natural elements, walking trails lead to the 16th-century Renaissance Château de Lacroix-Laval with stunning gardens. The family-friendly park features playgrounds and cycling-friendly paths. Trails like Allée des Terres Rouges and Allée du Grand Central offer picturesque routes, with the 5.1-km loop trail near Marcy-l'Étoile providing a scenic journey.

Getting there: Opt for the local 142 bus, running hourly and stopping outside the park entrance, for a convenient 23-minute journey. Alternatively, hourly trains take approximately 35 minutes to reach the far side of the park.

Address: 1171 Av. de Lacroix-Laval, 69280 Marcy-l'Étoile

5. Geneva (Switzerland)
Distance from Lyon: 149.6 km (1 hour, 58 minutes)

Overview: Geneva, an international city known for its diplomatic significance, is a mere 150 km from Lyon. Situated on the southern tip of Lake Geneva, the city boasts landmarks like the iconic water jet. Wander through the clean and classic architecture of the city, visit the Flower Clock, and explore the City Center shopping district. Geneva offers a rich cultural experience with museums such as the Patek Philippe Museum, Musée d'Art et d'Histoire, and Musée Ariana. Don't miss attractions like Place du Bourg-de-Four and Basilica Notre-Dame.

Getting there: Effortlessly travel from Lyon to Geneva with regular trains completing the journey in just under 2 hours. While buses are an option, trains provide a faster and more frequent connection.

6. Avignon
Distance from Lyon: 229.3 km (2 hours, 32 minutes)

Overview: Nestled along the Rhône River, the medieval city of Avignon is famed for the Palais de Papes, a grand Gothic palace and fortress that served as the official papal residence for a century. Explore the Romanesque Avignon Cathedral, featuring statues and tombs of 14th-century popes, along with religious artifacts at the chapel. Cross the iconic Pont d'Avignon, a medieval bridge with four arches and a surviving gatehouse. Visit the Musée du Petit Palais and Musée Lapidaire for Renaissance paintings, classical sculptures, and artifacts from ancient cultures. Admire the defensive stone walls, fortifications, and towers of the Remparts d'Avignon, and stroll the cobblestone streets of Rue des Teinturiers along the canal, home to charming cafés and restaurants.

Georgia Tucker

Getting there: Avignon is easily accessible from Lyon with hourly high-speed train connections, completing the journey in approximately 1 hour and 20 minutes.

7. Parc Naturel Régional des Volcans d'Auvergne
Distance from Lyon: 189.9 km (2 hours, 15 minutes)

Overview: Central France hosts the largest volcanic complex in Europe, known as Parc naturel régional des Volcans d'Auvergne. Encompassing 80 volcanoes across nearly 400,000 hectares, this regional natural park includes Monts Dore, Artense, Cézallier, and the ancestral Cantal massif. Explore hiking trails from Puy Mary to Puy de Dôme, offering diverse landscapes and volcanic formations. The region's volcanic stone contributed to notable structures in Clermont-Ferrand, such as the Cathédrale Notre-Dame-de-l'Assomption.

Trails: Popular trails include an 8-kilometer route near Mont-Dore and a 2-hour trail near Orcines, both showcasing the lush Chaîne des Puy with craters, lava domes, and cinder cones.

8. Vienne
Distance from Lyon: 33.6 km (44 minutes)

Overview: Situated 35 kilometers south of Lyon, Vienne sits at the confluence of the Gère and Rhône rivers. Once a major Roman center, Vienne preserves its ancient Roman heritage. Explore the Corinthian Temple of Augustus and Livia, dating back to the 1st century. The Archeological Gardens of Cybele feature ruins from ancient buildings, while the Vienne Ancient Roman Theatre offers a historic venue for events. Museums like Musée archéologique Saint-Pierre de Vienne and Museum of Fine Arts and Archeology of Vienne showcase the city's cultural richness. Don't miss the Saint Maurice Cathedral and the Abbaye de Saint-André-le-Bas de Vienne while strolling through the charming town.

Getting there: Enjoy a quick 30-minute train ride from Lyon to Vienne, with regular departures offering convenience for an easy day trip. Consider guided tours for a combination of Vienne exploration and wine-tasting experiences.

9. Bourg Saint Maurice
Distance from Lyon: 209.7 km (2 hours, 36 minutes)

Overview: Located near the Italian border, Bourg Saint Maurice is a haven for outdoor enthusiasts. The Les Arcs Ski Resort offers 425 kilometers of slopes with varying difficulty levels, surrounded by dense forests and scattered villages. The landscapes extend to the la Plagne area, overlook the Haute-Tarentaise, and lead to Mont-Blanc, Europe's highest peak. After outdoor activities, relax at the Spa Deep Nature – Les Sources de Marie, featuring hot tubs and saunas. Nama Springs, with mineral spring baths, massages, hammams, and saunas, provides another rejuvenating option. Experience exhilarating rafting with Arc Adventures Rafting Bourg Saint Maurice on the stunning river, guided by professional staff for both beginners and advanced individuals.

10. Macon
Distance from Lyon: 73 km (1 hour, 8 minutes)

Overview: Situated at the southern end of Burgundy along the River Saône, Macon charms with pastel-colored houses lining its riverfront. Notable churches include the 19th-century Église Saint Pierre, featuring three ports and twin steeples, and the remains of the Old Cathedral of Saint Vincent from the 11th to 14th centuries. Explore the city's oldest house, Maison de Bois, offering insights into its architectural past. The River Saône, connected by Pont Saint-Laurent, adds to the city's allure. Discover local history, archaeology, and art at the Musée des Ursulines, housed in a former 17th-century convent.

11. Grottes du Cerdon
Distance from Lyon: 88.4 km (1 hour, 3 minutes)

Overview: Northeast of Lyon, Grottes du Cerdon offers a unique weekend escape into the heart of wilderness. Descend into the underground world of the Cerdon Valley, exploring a prehistoric shelter adorned with stalactites and stalagmites dating back nearly 10,000 years. The guided trail, lasting about an hour and thirty minutes, takes you through prehistoric workshops where you can engage in activities like fire-making, spear throwing, crafting natural ocher paint, and making jewelry and pottery. The underground path is well-landscaped, marked, and lit; however, bring warm clothing and comfortable shoes due to temperature drops and walking involved.

Getting there: Given infrequent public transport, driving is the recommended option for this day trip from Lyon to Grottes de Cerdon.

12. Aix-les-Bains
Distance from Lyon: 113.8 km (1 hour, 21 minutes)

Overview: Aix-les-Bains, situated in the Savoie region of France on Lake Bourget, is a classic thermal spa town. The historical Casino Grand Cercle Aix-les-Bains, known for its stunning art decor and frescoes, features a smart casino with gaming tables, a piano bar, nightclub, and restaurant. Spa Parenthesis Aix Les Bains offers a complete aqua-relaxation area with a jacuzzi, heated swimming pool, sauna, hammam, and relaxing treatments. The Temple of Diana's ruins, dating back to Roman rule, and the emblematic Château de la Roche du Roi, a picturesque castle on a hillside in the southern part of the city, are must-visit landmarks.

13. Grenoble
Distance from Lyon: 111.6 km (1 hour, 18 minutes)

Overview: Nestled between the Isère and Drac rivers, Grenoble is renowned for its nuclear physics and microelectronics research centers. The city offers excellent terrain for winter sports, with the Téléphérique providing a panoramic view from the city center to the 18th-century Fort de la Bastille. Explore various museums, including Musée de Grenoble for fine arts, Musée dauphinois for ethnography and archaeology, and the Museum of the Resistance and Deportation of Isère. Historic buildings like Eglise Saint Louis and Cathédrale Notre-Dame add to Grenoble's charm.

14. Perouges
Distance from Lyon: 40.2 km (36 minutes)

Overview: Perouges, an authentic medieval town overlooking the Ain River, remains unspoiled by touristy structures. Its half-timbered stone houses and cobblestone roads offer a picturesque setting. The old Church of Saint Mary Magdalene and its fortress provide insight into the city's history. Hostellerie Du Vieux Perouges, a charming restaurant, serves local delicacies like Galette de Perouges and Pérougeoise. Musée du Vieux Pérouges, with beautiful gardens and panoramic views, houses a collection of art, artifacts, and armor.

15. Gorges de la Loire

Distance from Lyon: 79.2 km (1 hour, 9 minutes)

Overview: Gorges de la Loire, a 4000-hectare reserve around the Loire River, offers biodiversity and hiking trails. Explore medieval towns like Aurec-sur-Loire along the loop of the Loire and Chambles, a steep village with beautiful views. Visit the old castle of Essalois overlooking the Grangent dam lake. Boating along the river allows you to see princely estates, including the Château de Lavoûte. The Gorges de la Loire is renowned for its 3-star campsite with 143 pitches, surrounded by hills, wild meadows, and the river, providing opportunities for various outdoor activities.

BEST OUTDOOR ADVENTURES IN AND AROUND LYON
Embark on an Active Weekend in Lyon

Lyon, the bustling capital of the Rhône-Alpes region in southeastern France, offers fantastic opportunities to enjoy the outdoors and breathe in fresh air. Whether you prefer a leisurely stroll or more adventurous pursuits, France's third-largest city has it all.

For those keen on staying close to the city, options range from exploring the waterways to soaring high in the sky on a helicopter sightseeing tour. Lyon also serves as an excellent base for day trips to the nearby mountains. If you're seeking outdoor activities, these 10 best adventures in and around Lyon are a must-try.

1. Grand Parc Miribel Jonage
Bike, hike, fish, golf, and more in a pristine setting

Located in Vaulx-en-Velin, just 15 minutes from Lyon, Grand Parc Miribel Jonage is an outdoor enthusiast's haven, offering a plethora of activities on both land and lake. Spanning 2,200 hectares between the Miribel and Jonage canals, this expansive park features unspoiled nature, including four beaches. Rent bikes, stand-up paddleboards, or other equipment from L'atol centre by Eaux Bleus Lake, or enjoy the tennis courts and 9-hole golf course.

Water activities abound at Grand Parc Miribel Jonage, from kayaking to sailing lessons and fishing. Cyclists and runners can explore scenic trails surrounded by lush greenery.

Location: Chem. de la Bletta, 69120 Vaulx-en-Velin, France

Open: 24/7

Phone: +33 4 78 80 56 20

2. Les Grottes de la Balme

Embark on a day trip to discover an underground world of caves

Les Grottes de la Balme, situated a little over 2 hours from Lyon in Isère, offers a captivating underground adventure through stunning caves. Explore a rich mineral landscape featuring striking stalagmites and stalactites, along with colorful pools of water.

As you navigate the caves, encounter a marvelous main room and, if lucky, catch a glimpse of bats. The site includes a maze, and you can delve into its intriguing history, including its use as a hideout for a notorious smuggler.

Georgia Tucker

3. Animal Park of Courzieu (Parc de Courzieu)
Learn and have fun in this 'wild' world

Less than an hour from Lyon in the town of Courzieu near the Monts du Lyonnais, the Animal Park of Courzieu invites you to explore a preserved natural area teeming with diverse flora and fauna. The park is a sanctuary for grey and arctic wolves, marmots, and birds of prey.

Discover these fascinating creatures through animal encounters and feedings. Additionally, enjoy nature trail walks and special events, such as nights under the stars and tree climbing.

Location: Parc de Courzieu, 1865 route du parc, Montmain la Côte, 69690 Courzieu, France

Open: Daily from 10 am to 6 pm

Phone: +33 4 74 70 96 10

4. City Adventure - Lyon Sainte Foy
Entertainment for the Whole Family

City Adventure - Lyon Sainte Foy offers attractions suitable for all age groups within its woodland theme park. Situated a mere 15 minutes from the city center, this family-oriented destination nestled in a century-old forest provides rides, nature trails, and outdoor activities. Engage in unique experiences like The Hut's Pathway, an elevated footbridge in the trees, or take on the challenge of Mission: Ultimate within the canopy.

At City Adventure - Lyon Sainte Foy, you'll find tranquil spots for relaxation or picnics. Following a break, explore additional attractions such as the Family Slide, The Hut (a hanging hut in the trees), Gigaball, and The Little Trapper's Path accordion bridge designed for kids.

Location: Chem. de la Croix Berthet, 69110 Sainte-Foy-lès-Lyon, France

5. Pilat Natural Regional Park
A Expansive Nature Sanctuary to Discover

Pilat Natural Regional Park presents a picturesque setting for outdoor enthusiasts. Located less than 50 minutes by car from Lyon, this protected mountainous expanse in the Auvergne-Rhône-Alpes region spans 65,000 hectares. Adventurers will find a variety of ways to explore the park, including paragliding.

Perfect for year-round visits, Pilat Natural Regional Park boasts numerous hiking trails offering diverse scenery. Mountain bikers can traverse 1,500 km of trails suitable for every skill level, with the Crêt de la Perdrix passage as a standout feature. Winter brings opportunities for sledding and skiing, while nature workshops and family activities are available throughout the year.

Location: Col de l'Œillon, 42410 Pélussin, France

Open: 24/7

Phone: +33 4 74 87 52 00

6. Planfoy Via Ferata
Climbing Adventure with Breathtaking Views

Georgia Tucker

Via Ferrata of Planfoy provides an unparalleled mountaineering experience catering to all skill levels. Located just 50 minutes from Lyon in the regional natural park of Pilat, this protected climbing route offers stunning views, including glimpses of the Gouffre d'Enfer waterfalls.

Featuring two climbing routes, Via Ferrata of Planfoy offers guided instruction for those interested. The children's route is designed as an engaging introduction to climbing for kids aged 6 and older, complete with fun features like footbridges. The adult's course takes you along a ridge above the dam of Rochetaillé, delivering a memorable mountaineering experience.

Location: 42660 Planfoy, France *Open:* 24/7

7. Lyon River Cruises
Discover the Cityscape from the Water

Embarking on Lyon river cruises offers a splendid opportunity to admire the landscapes of France's third-largest city. Whether opting for a guided tour or navigating the waters with a rented canoe, various companies provide diverse experiences. Lyon, positioned along the Rhône and Saône Rivers, unfolds its scenic beauty during these excursions.

Among the Lyon River cruise operators, Les Bateaux Lyonnais stands out, offering sightseeing excursions encompassing the Renaissance District, Old Lyon, and Ile Barbe—a serene green haven. For those inclined towards canoeing or stand-up paddle adventures, Lyon Canoë provides rentals along with expert guidance.

8. Vercors Massif
A Fascinating Canyoning Destination

Vercors Massif, an enchanting mountain plateau, is nestled within the Vercors Natural Regional Park, boasting over a dozen canyons to explore. Located a little over 2.5 hours from Lyon, between Isère and Drôme in the French pre-Alps, the park makes for an ideal day trip.

For beginners in canyoning, Vercors Massif within the Vercors Natural Regional Park offers manageable descents like Les Carmes and Le Betton. Experienced enthusiasts can delve into challenging experiences such as Le Ruzand and the upper section of Les Ecouges, featuring a thrilling 68-meter waterfall abseil. Numerous outfitters provide canyoning experiences.

Location: 38250 Corrençon-en-Vercors, France

9. Lyon Helicopter Tours
Aerial Views of Lyon's Splendor

Lyon helicopter tours provide a breathtaking bird's-eye perspective of this beautiful French city, enhancing your holiday experience. For those contemplating an exploration of France's third-largest city and its scenic environs from high above, various travel companies offer captivating experiences.

Consider the helicopter tour offered by Manawa, featuring a flight over historic castles in the nearby Beaujolais region. Alternatively, Mont Blanc Helicoptere provides a panoramic flight over Lyon, showcasing not only the city but also the surrounding mountains and vineyards.

10. Monts d'Or
Traverse Scenic Trails in this Majestic Massif

Monts d'Or invites you to embark on a picturesque journey through the Lyon metropolitan countryside. Several trails wind through the landscapes beneath the Monts d'Or massif. The 3-mile Saint-Romain-au-Mont-d'Or route offers a leisurely stroll with views of the Salagon hamlet and the remnants of a Roman aqueduct.

Opt for the 3.5-mile Collonges-au-Mont-d'Or path for panoramic views of the Saône valley and the Dombes plateau. Exploring the Poleymieux-au-Mont-d'Or route reveals stone huts and panoramic vistas of forests and valleys.

CHAPTER FOUR: SIGHTSEEING

ICONIC BUILDINGS AND PLACES IN LYON

Discover Lyon's Most Celebrated Landmarks. Lyon, a captivating French city, offers a wealth of attractions for travelers, particularly those intrigued by iconic landmarks. With a history dating back to the Roman era, Lyon boasts a rich tapestry of buildings and landmarks spanning various historical periods.

For an enriching Lyon experience, it's beneficial to identify the key landmarks and structures to prioritize during your visit. Here's a curated list of the city's iconic buildings and places:

1. Fourvière Basilica

The Fourvière Basilica, an imposing church devoted to the Virgin Mary, boasts a distinctive architectural style that blends Romanesque and Byzantine influences. Marked by four main towers

Georgia Tucker

and a bell tower crowned with a gilded Virgin Mary statue, the basilica stands across from Fourvière Station.

Inside, marvel at its aesthetic brilliance showcased through captivating stained glass and intricate mosaics. Locals affectionately refer to it as the "upside-down elephant" due to its resemblance to the creature's body with the towers as its legs.

Positioned atop the site of the ancient Roman forum of Trajan, the Basilica of Notre-Dame de Fourvière is a minor basilica with historical significance. Dedicated to the Virgin Mary, it is believed to have protected the city from the bubonic plague in 1643, a Cholera epidemic in 1932, and invasion in 1870.

Key Highlights:

- The Choir of the Basilica, featuring a children's choir

- Hosting Radio Fourvière antennas

- Exquisite mosaics and stained glass

- The reputed crypt of Saint Joseph

- The Shrine of Notre-Dame de Fourvière, a pilgrimage site since 1170

Visitors are encouraged to show due respect as the basilica functions as a Roman Catholic church. While tours are available, it's advised to explore on days and times when Mass is not in session. The basilica is committed to accessibility, offering assistance to individuals with mobility challenges and hearing-impaired visitors.

Location: 8 Pl. de Fourvière, 69005 Lyon, France

Opening Hours: Monday–Sunday from 7 am to 8 pm

Phone: +33 (0)4 78 25 13 01

2. Bartholdi Fountain

The Bartholdi Fountain stands as a remarkable lead-made structure portraying a woman seated on a chariot, guiding four powerful horses. Symbolizing the embodiment of France, the woman represents the nation, while the horses symbolize its most renowned rivers. Although the statue maintains overall symmetry, each element possesses a distinct and unique character. Crafted from lead and supported by an iron frame, it holds the classification of a historic monument. Located at Place des Terreaux in Lyon's 1st Arrondissement.

Location: Pl. des Terreaux, 69001 Lyon, France

Open: 24/7

Phone: +33 (0)4 72 77 69 69

Georgia Tucker

3. Place Bellecour

La Place Bellecour stands as Lyon's central historic city square, steeped in centuries of history and featuring iconic statuary and sculptures. With origins dating back to Roman times, the square served various purposes, evolving from a vineyard to a military encampment. A UNESCO World Heritage Site, it has borne different names throughout history, including Place Royale, Place Louis-le-Grand, Place de la Fédération, Place de l'Égalité, Placé Bonaparte, and finally, Place Bellecour. Among Europe's largest open pedestrian squares, it is a hub of social activity.

Highlights:

- Central equestrian statue of Louis XIV

- Statues representing the Saône and the Rhône

- Stone Watchmen and the statue of Antoine de Saint Exupéry with the Little Prince

The square hosts various events, including book fairs, public concerts, demonstrations, and a winter transformation featuring a public ice rink and a 60-meter Ferris wheel. During Pentecost weekend, a pétanque competition takes place.

Additional Information: Place Bellecour serves as the literal center of Lyon, denoted as kilometer 0, from which all city distances are measured. Radiating from the square are four main thoroughfares leading to the opera house, boutique shops, cafes, restaurants, and hotels. A vibrant meeting place for locals and visitors, including young professionals and lawyers. Nearby, Decitre, an international bookshop, attracts those seeking English-language texts. The Lyon Tourist Office is conveniently situated steps away.

Location: Place, 69002 Lyon, France

Open: 24/7

Phone: +33 (0)4 72 77 69 69

4. Cathédrale Saint-Jean-Baptiste

The Lyon Cathedral, officially known as Cathédrale Saint-Jean-Baptiste, stands as the ecclesiastical seat of the Archbishop of Lyon and is renowned for its exceptional architectural beauty. Erected on the grounds of a former 6th-century church, the cathedral's construction spanned from 1180 to 1476.

A prominent attraction for both Catholics and secular visitors, the cathedral boasts remarkable features, including its medieval Gothic architecture showcased in the nave and façade. The Romanesque design of the interior apse and choir adds to its historical significance. Notably, the Bourbon Chapel within is hailed as a masterpiece of 15th-century sculpture.

Highlights:

- The Gothic architecture of the nave and façade

Georgia Tucker

- Romanesque design in the apse and choir

- Historic crosses from the Second Council of Lyon in 1274

- The renowned Lyon Astronomical Clock, a 14th-century marvel standing 9 meters tall, featuring automated figures and celestial indications

The cathedral hosts the annual Festival of Lights in December, marked by captivating choreographed lighting displays. Situated in the heart of Vieux Lyon, the city's old town neighborhood, it remains a spiritual hub and a cultural landmark.

Additional Information: While serving as a major tourist attraction, Cathédrale Saint-Jean-Baptiste is an active Catholic Church and the seat of the diocesan Archbishop. As a site of spiritual significance, visitors are urged to maintain a respectful and quiet demeanor, especially during Mass. Guided tours, available in various languages, including English, provide insights into the cathedral's rich history.

Adjacent to the cathedral, the Café de la Cathédrale offers a convenient spot for refreshments, while the northern side features an archaeological garden showcasing ruins from the 4th to 6th centuries. It's advisable to note that the area tends to be crowded in the afternoons and on weekends.

Location: Pl. Saint-Jean, 69005 Lyon, France

Open: Monday–Friday from 8:15 am to 7:45 pm, Saturday from 8:15 am to 7 pm, Sunday from 8 am to 7 pm

Phone: +33 (0)6 60 83 53 97

5. Gallo-Roman Theatre (Teatro Galo-Romano)

The Gallo-Roman Theatre in Lyon, constructed approximately between 15 B.C.E. and the 2nd century C.E., stands as an architectural marvel designed to accommodate 10,000 spectators within its expansive 180-meter diameter circumference. Positioned on the slope of a hill, the theatre utilizes the natural terrain for amphitheater-style seating. In ancient times, it hosted various performances, including plays and dance presentations.

Highlights: One of the significant highlights of the Gallo-Roman Theatre is the renowned Nuits de Fourviére (Nights of Fourviére) festival, held annually since 1946. This summer event encompasses theatre, music, dance, circus acts, and film presentations, attracting thousands of spectators. Notably, the theatre plays a central role in this festival, drawing well over 100,000 attendees. Outside of festival times, visitors can explore and capture images of the stage, Roman pillars, seating, and meticulously maintained surrounding gardens. It offers an opportunity to tread the same stage where Roman performers once showcased their talents.

Additional Information: The theatre, often referred to as the "Large Theatre," stands adjacent to the Odeon, another ancient Roman theatre of smaller scale, both actively participating in the annual festival. The Odeon was originally designed for musical performances and speeches. Guided tours are available for individuals and groups, providing insights into the historical significance of the site. Visitors with disabilities can access most areas, and those requiring accommodation can obtain complimentary audio guides and free entry for two accompanying companions.

Location: Rue de l'Antiquaille, 69005 Lyon, France

Open: Hours vary by show

Phone: +33 (0)4 72 38 49 30

6. Lyon Opera House (Opera Nouvel)

The Lyon Opera House, also known as Opera Nouvel, stands as a remarkable architectural achievement housing the National Opéra of Lyon. Originally built in the 19th century as a rectangular Italian-style structure with a horseshoe-shaped auditorium, it underwent transformative additions by the latest architect, Jean Nouvel. The contemporary design features a striking steel and glass barrel vault atop and expanded subterranean space, tripling the interior size. Located on the east side of Pentes de la Croix Rousse, south of Place Louis Pradel.

Location: 1 Pl. de la Comédie, 69001 Lyon, France

Phone: +33 (0)4 69 85 54 54

7. Canuts Painted Wall

The Canuts Painted Wall stands as an expansive mural portraying a vivid landscape, capturing the hyper-realistic essence of everyday life in the La Croix-Rousse neighborhood. Remarkable in its intricate details, the mural invites viewers to engage in prolonged observation, attempting to discern every nuance.

Details: Situated near the heart of the La Croix-Rousse neighborhood at the crossroads of Bd des Canuts and Rue Denfert-Rochereau.

Location: 36 Bd des Canuts, 69004 Lyon, France

Open: 24/7

Phone: +33 (0)4 78 50 44 57

8. Parc de la Tête d'Or

Parc de la Tête d'Or in Lyon stands as one of the largest urban parks in France, providing a sanctuary with attractions including a zoo, lake, gardens, pony rides, and a miniature railroad. This park offers an escape into the tranquility of nature, allowing visitors to explore kilometers of trails, engage in recreational activities, enjoy picnics, or simply relax.

Highlights: Established in 1857, the park has evolved with added features, from expansive gardens to captivating greenhouses. Noteworthy attractions include glass greenhouses with botanical gardens dating back to the late 18th century, boasting a diverse array of plant species worldwide. The rose gardens showcase 30,000 bushes representing 350 distinct rose varieties, while the zoo, the second-largest in France, features 400 animals spanning 64 species.

Dozens of trails cater to hiking, jogging, and biking enthusiasts, and a boating lake provides a serene water experience. For families, the park offers pony rides, swings, miniature train rides, pedal cars, mini boats, and a classic merry-go-round.

Additional Information: The Parc de la Tête d'Or is conveniently located a short walk northeast from the city center, situated across the Rhone behind the Opera, approximately a 15-minute walk. Accessible via public transportation, including metro and bus, or by personal vehicle with nearby parking options.

Much of the park is designed to accommodate individuals with disabilities, featuring flat and easily navigable paved trails. An online map assists in locating preferred activities, ensuring a seamless exploration. With extended hours, the park remains a family-friendly destination catering to diverse interests.

Location: 69006 Lyon, France

Open: Monday–Sunday from 6.30 am to 10.30 pm

Phone: +33 (0)4 72 69 47 60

9. Hôtel Dieu

Hôtel Dieu stands as an impressive hospital structure along the river, with roots tracing back to medieval times when it was inaugurated in the mid-15th century. Within its walls, visitors encounter the Musee des Hospices Civils, a permanent exhibition narrating the history of medical practices.

Upon approaching the building, one is greeted by a captivating dome and an array of windows extending in both directions from the central spire. Positioned on the east side of Place Bellecour, the edifice graces the banks of the Rhône.

Location: 1 Pl. de l'Hôpital, 69002 Lyon, France

Open: Daily from 10 am to 8 pm

10. Quartier Saint-Jean and Quartier Saint-Georges (Old Town)

In Lyon's evocative Quartier Saint-Jean, one can immerse themselves in the historic charm of Vieux Lyon, the Old Town. This medieval district, situated north of the cathedral, boasts narrow cobblestone streets and serene courtyards.

Commence your exploration around Rue du Boeuf and the scenic Place Neuve Saint-Jean, a square adorned with traditional restaurants. Meander through pedestrian avenues like Rue Saint-Jean and Rue des Trois-Maries, encountering inviting shops, crêperies, bouchons, and cozy cafés.

Continue your journey until reaching the Hôtel de Gadagne at the Place du Petit Collège. This 16th-century mansion hosts two noteworthy museums: The Musée d'Histoire de Lyon, illustrating the city's history from antiquity to the 20th century, and the Musée des Arts de La Marionnette, showcasing puppets from around the world.

A brief walk from the Gadagne museums leads to Théâtre Le Guignol de Lyon (2 Rue Louis Carrand), where the Compagnie M.A. marionette company performs. For another marionette spectacle, head to Quartier Saint-Georges at the Théâtre La Maison de Guignol puppet theater (Place de la Trinité, 2 Montée du Gourguillon). Both theaters offer performances in French, so check the schedule in advance.

Near the Cathédrale Saint-Jean-Baptiste, you'll find the Café du Soleil (2 Rue Saint-Georges), an excellent spot for an authentic Lyonnais meal. Steps away from the cathedral stands La Maison du Chamarier (37 Rue Saint-Jean), a classified Historical Monument exhibiting the transition from Flamboyant Gothic to Renaissance architecture.

Adjacent to the cathedral is La Maison de Guignol theater, and a short stroll away is A la Marquise (37 rue Saint Jean at Rue Bombarde), a historic pâtisserie with a refined tea room. This esteemed boutique serves classic French pastries and Lyonnaise specialties, such as tarte à la praline and bugnes, and is open Wednesday through Sunday from 9 am until 7:30 pm.

Note: *All puppet performances are in French, and it's advisable to check the schedule beforehand.*

Georgia Tucker

Café du Soleil Location: 2 Rue Saint-Georges, Lyon

La Maison du Chamarier Location: 37 Rue Saint-Jean, Lyon

A la Marquise Location: 37 rue Saint Jean at Rue Bombarde, Lyon

11. Museum of Gallo-Roman Civilization

Lyon occupies the grounds of the ancient Roman city, Lugdunum, established in 43 BC, serving as the capital of Gaul. The Museum of Gallo-Roman Civilization, also known as the Museum of Archaeology, exhibits objects from the Gallo-Roman era, showcasing vases, gravestones, mosaics, statues, coins, and ceramics.

The artifacts on display come from excavations within Lugdunum and nearby Roman archaeological sites, such as Saint-Romain-en-Gal and Vienne. Renowned for its extensive and diverse collection, highlights include a monumental sculpture of Hercules, exquisite marble work from ancient baths, and a spectacular 100-square-meter mosaic illustrating themes related to the God of Oceans.

Situated next to an archaeological site boasting the oldest ancient ruins in France, including two Roman theaters, the museum's surroundings feature the Grand Théâtre (15 BC) for tragedies and comedies, the Odéon for musical performances, and the foundations of a temple devoted to the Goddess Cybele.

Address: Museum, 17 Rue Cléberg, Lyon; Archaeological Site, 6 Rue de l'Antiquaille, Lyon

12. Gourmet Restaurants, Culinary Boutiques, and Cooking Classes

Lyon holds the esteemed title of the capital of French gastronomy, making it a must-visit for indulging in regional cuisine. Local delights include hearty dishes like steak, lamb stew, roast chicken with morels, and poached eggs in red wine sauce. A unique specialty, "quenelles," a type of dumpling made with ground fish in a rich cream sauce, adds to the culinary allure.

For an authentic experience, explore "Bouchons Lyonnais," family-run bistros offering simple yet delectable meals, showcasing classic regional specialties. Renowned restaurants, including those created by Paul Bocuse, enrich Lyon's culinary landscape. The Presqu'île district boasts Brasserie Le Nord for Lyonnais specialties and Brasserie Le Sud for Mediterranean cuisine, while Brasserie L'Ouest on Quai du Commerce offers a blend of classic French and international dishes.

For an elegant dining affair, consider the historic Grand Café des Négociants (1 Place Francisque Régaud) in the Presqu'île district. Dating back to 1864, this brasserie delivers traditional Lyonnaise cuisine in an opulent Second Empire dining room. The Grand Café des Négociants was initially a meeting place for silk merchants and diamond vendors, evident in its luxurious ambiance.

Gourmet enthusiasts can also explore renowned chocolate boutiques like Palomas and Boutique Voisin and discover high-end culinary items at Giraudet, which also provides cooking classes. A L'Olivier offers the finest French olive oils, and Les Halles de Lyon - Paul Bocuse is a covered marketplace with over 50 shops and restaurants, presenting an array of regional products, from charcuterie and locally made cheese to fresh bread, truffles, and chocolate bonbons.

Note: All locations mentioned are within Lyon, France.

13. Croix-Rousse Hill

Situated on the slopes of Croix-Rousse hill, this historic district played a pivotal role in weaving during the early 19th century. Characterized by its steep streets, the neighborhood boasts picturesque curves and staircases.

A distinctive feature is its array of traboules, concealed passages weaving through courtyards, buildings (including residences), and pedestrian staircases. In the 19th century, silk workers utilized these covered alleyways to transport their fabrics. Exploring this area offers tourists the opportunity to uncover architectural marvels within the winding streets and concealed traboules.

Traboules can be found starting at 9 Place Colbert to 14 Bis Montée Saint Sébastien, from 20 Rue Imbert Colomès to 55 Rue des Tables Claudiennes, and from 30 Rue Burdeau to 19 Rue René Leynaud (Passage Thiaffait). While these traboules are open to the public, visitors are encouraged to maintain quietude out of respect for the residents.

A notable attraction in the vicinity is the Maison des Canuts (House of Silk Workers) at 10/12 Rue d'Ivry. This compact museum is dedicated to the art of silk creation, offering insights into the invention of the Jacquard loom and hosting hand-weaving demonstrations on traditional looms.

14. Presqu'île District

The Presqu'île district in Lyon resembles an island within the river, distinguished by its captivating architecture and grand town squares. Noteworthy is the Place des Terreaux, featuring F.A. Bartholdi's fountain portraying the triumphant chariot of the Garonne River. Four diligently sculpted horses represent the four rivers flowing into the ocean.

Lyon's Hôtel de Ville (Town Hall) graces the east side of the square, originally constructed between 1646 and 1672 and later rebuilt in Baroque style by Jules Hardouin-Mansart after a fire.

Another monumental structure in the area is the Palais de la Bourse et du Commerce on Rue de la République. Despite its Renaissance architectural style, this 19th-century construction houses historical

Georgia Tucker

significance. South of the Palais de la Bourse, tourists encounter the Eglise Saint-Bonaventure, a former Franciscan church dating back to the 14th-15th centuries.

Place Bellecour, Lyon's premier square between the Rhône and Saône Rivers, features an equestrian statue of Louis XIV sculpted by Lyon-native F. Lemot. Elegant 19th-century buildings line the east and west sides, offering a view of the Fourvière hill from the north.

A short stroll from Place Bellecour leads to the Hôtel-Dieu de Lyon, a splendid 17th-century structure once serving as a hospital. Another charming square, Place Carnot, accessible via Rue Victor-Hugo, boasts an expansive monument to the Republic crafted in 1890.

15. Museum of Fabrics and Decorative Arts

Nestled within an 18th-century mansion are two exceptional museums: the Fabric Museum and the Museum of Decorative Arts. The Fabric Museum, known as Musée des Tissus, is a distinctive institution where visitors can explore the captivating history of Lyon's silk trade, dating back to the Renaissance.

The collection boasts rare fragments of clothing from the 13th and 14th centuries, exquisite 18th-century tapestries, and more modern pieces from the 19th and 20th centuries. Notable displays include a splendid silk dress worn by Empress Josephine and a pleated tunic from Egypt's 5th Dynasty era, dating to around 2,500 BC.

Adjacent to this, the Museum of Decorative Arts, or Musée des Arts Décoratifs, presents a diverse array of decorative artwork, encompassing faïence, paper, wood, and various materials. The exhibits include small religious sculptures, Japanese figurines, Italian majolica pieces, vintage dinnerware, antique furniture, and clocks. These items are thoughtfully arranged in realistic settings, providing cultural context, and some rooms feature opulent decor, offering visitors a glimpse into a bygone era.

Address: 34 Rue de la Charité, Lyon

16. Centre d'Histoire de la Résistance et de la Déportation

Lyon earned the moniker "Capital of the Resistance" during World War II due to its robust opposition to the Nazi regime. The Center for the History of Resistance and Deportation occupies the building once used by the Head of the Gestapo in Lyon and is now dedicated to commemorating the victims who were confined in the cellars of this historic structure.

Open to the public from Tuesday through Sunday, the History Center serves as a museum narrating the experiences of deportees, hidden children, and resistance members during World War II. The permanent exhibition outlines key events of the war, particularly the years of occupied France.

A documentary film about the trial of Klaus Barbie, the SS officer who led the Gestapo in Lyon, is screened at the center. Featuring eyewitness accounts and trial excerpts, an audio guide aids visitors in navigating the historical information presented through videos, photos, and written documents.

The center's mission is to honor citizens in the resistance and pay tribute to the memories of deportation victims. Continuously updating its content, the center actively seeks WWII eyewitnesses to share their stories.

Address: Espace Berthelot, 14 Avenue Berthelot, Lyon

17. Basilique Notre-Dame de Fourvière

Located majestically on the Colline de Fourvière, the hill overseeing Vieux Lyon, the Basilica of Notre-Dame de Fourvière stands tall at 130 meters above the Saône River. Accessible via funiculars ascending the hill, this striking church was erected between 1872 and 1884 following the Franco-Prussian War. The people of Lyon had pledged to establish a Marian sanctuary if their city was spared.

The Basilica exhibits a captivating blend of Gothic and Byzantine architectural styles, adorned with a lavishly decorated interior. Take time to appreciate the opulent mosaics and paintings within the sanctuary. Upon exploring the interior, ascend the northeast tower for breathtaking views of Lyon's cityscape and its surroundings.

For panoramic vistas, visit the Esplanade de Fourvière, located on the left side of the Basilica, offering a sweeping outlook onto Lyon. The views extend to the Croix-Rousse and Terreaux districts, the Quartier Saint-Jean downhill, and the Place Bellecour on the right.

Address: Place de Fourvière, Lyon

18. Cathedral of Saint-John the Baptist

Constructed in the 12th century, the magnificent Cathedral of Saint-John is celebrated for its 13th- to 14th-century stained-glass windows. The grand rose window, dating back to 1392, bathes the interior in a vibrant array of colors. Primarily Romanesque with a Late Gothic facade, the cathedral boasts an intriguing astronomical clock crafted by Nicolas Lippius in 1598.

A notable feature is the impressive bell, "Anne-Marie de la Primatiale," cast in 1622, ranking among the largest ever made and rung exclusively on Catholic feast days. To appreciate a picturesque view of the cathedral from a distance, visit the embankment near the Pont Bonaparte, providing a perspective of the soaring twin towers.

The cathedral welcomes the public for prayer and meditation daily. Weekday opening hours are from 8:15 am to 7:45 pm, and on weekends from 8 am to 7 pm. Mass is conducted Monday through Saturday at 9 am, with an additional service on Fridays at 7 pm. On Sundays, Mass takes place at 8:30 am and 10:30 am.

Address: Place Saint-Jean, Lyon

19. Basilica - Abbey of Saint-Martin d'Ainay

The Basilica - Abbey of Saint-Martin d'Ainay stands as Lyon's oldest church, dating back to the 11th century. It occupies the site of a 4th-century Roman temple, later replaced by a 9th-century Carolingian church. Originally part of a 6th-century Benedictine abbey, this structure is a splendid representation of Romanesque architecture. Notable features include four classical columns, a 12th-century mosaic pavement in the choir, and 19th-century gilded paintings by Lyon artist Hippolyte Flandrin.

Address: Place d'Ainay or 11 Rue Bourgelat, Lyon

20. Cultural Performances

Situated on the Place de la Comédie, the Opéra de Lyon is a lavish 19th-century opera house adorned with a majestic dome. Renovated by Jean Nouvel, the building's size was tripled using modern architectural techniques. The Opéra de Lyon hosts a diverse range of performances, including opera, dance, and classical music concerts.

Guided tours of the Opéra de Lyon are available on Wednesdays and Saturdays at 1 pm and Thursdays at 5:30 pm. Conducted in French, these 90-minute tours require advance reservation and can be booked online, by phone, or at the Opéra de Lyon ticket office. Groups can arrange visits Monday through Saturday (at 1 pm or 3 pm) by contacting the theater in advance.

The Théâtre des Célestins (4 Rue Charles Dullin) is a stunning Neoclassical theater constructed in 1881. Boasting an exquisite Italian-style auditorium, it features one of Europe's most beautiful ceilings and opulent gilded décor. The Célestins Theater showcases dramatic performances in French, spanning classical repertory to contemporary plays. Outside of performances, the theater is accessible to the public only on specific days for guided tours.

22. Mural of Famous People from Lyon

Along Quai Saint Vincent, an 800-square-meter mural showcases 31 renowned individuals from Lyon, featuring 25 historical figures and six contemporary personalities. Created by the Cité de la Création organization in 1994-1995, the mural includes a depiction of Paul Bocuse in front of the "Le Pot Beaujolais" restaurant.

Address: 49 Quai Saint Vincent and 2 Rue de la Martinière

23. Aquarium de Lyon

Established in 2002 and renovated in 2010, the Lyon Aquarium is dedicated to educating the public on marine ecosystems and environmental issues related to the ocean. The aquarium features tanks representing various ocean zones, including tropical and temperate waters.

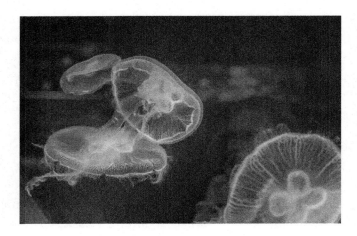

Through exhibits highlighting coral reefs and unique marine species, the Lyon Aquarium aims to raise awareness about the importance of preserving biodiversity. The aquarium is open Wednesday through Sunday from 10:30 am until 6:30 pm.

Address: 7 Rue Stéphane Déchant, La Mulatière

Official site: https://www.aquariumlyon.fr/en/

Tips and Tours: How to Make the Most of Your Visit to Lyon

When exploring a city as diverse as Lyon, opting for an organized tour can greatly enhance your experience. Guided by a knowledgeable local, you can effortlessly navigate through top tourist attractions, immersing yourself in the city's historical charm and cultural wonders. Below are recommended tours encompassing visits to Vieux Lyon (the Old Town) and other essential landmarks:

City Highlights Exploration: Hop-On Hop-Off Bus Tour: Ensure you don't miss any major sights with a comprehensive bus tour, making stops at over a dozen attractions, including museums, parks, and historic monuments.

Lyon Guided City Tour by Electric Tuk-Tuk: For a personalized touch, indulge in a one or two-hour private guided tour via Electric Tuk-Tuk, covering Lyon's key highlights like Place Bellecour and the Colline de Fourvière.

Vieux Lyon Exploration: Storytelling Walking Tour of Old Lyon: Stroll through the narrow, winding streets and ancient alleyways of the Old Town, transported back in time. A knowledgeable guide will share captivating stories of Renaissance-era inhabitants, bringing the city's intriguing past to vivid life.

Lyon City Tram to Colline de la Croix-Rousse: Explore the charming Colline de la Croix-Rousse district through the Lyon City Tram, which includes a guided tour by a mini-train, providing a delightful and informative excursion.

These tours offer a delightful blend of historical insights and contemporary exploration, ensuring a fulfilling visit to Lyon.

BEST MUSEUMS AND ART GALLERIES IN LYON

Lyon, with its profound history and vibrant culture, boasts some of the most remarkable and awe-inspiring art globally. The city's museums delve into its Roman roots and showcase diverse artistic expressions that have evolved through the ages.

During your visit to Lyon, a plethora of museums awaits exploration, each offering a unique lens into the city's narrative. Here, we present the top 10 museums in Lyon, inviting you to embark on an enriching journey of knowledge and discovery.

1. Museum of Confluences
Unraveling Science and Anthropology in Contemporary Settings

The Musée des Confluences, a sprawling institution in Lyon, beckons with its exploration of natural science, anthropology, earth sciences, and the arts. Housed in a striking ultramodern structure, this museum spans 44 meters in height, 150 meters in length, and 83 meters in width, encompassing a vast exhibition space of 6,500 square meters. Opened in 2014, it boasts nine exhibitions, four permanent and five rotating, exemplifying the deconstructivist architectural style—a floating cloud of crystal, glass, and stainless steel.

Highlights of Musée des Confluences in Lyon:

- ***Origins:*** Explores the birth of the universe, evolution, and diverse origin theories.

- ***Species:*** Examines the interconnectedness of humans and animals.

- ***Societies:*** Investigates the building and development of communities.

- ***Eternities:*** Explores how societies perceive the meaning of life.

The museum also hosts five rotating temporary exhibits, delving into focused aspects of science, history, and the arts.

Additional Information: The expansive exhibition space requires ample time for exploration, so plan accordingly. Multilingual maps in French, English, Italian, Spanish, and German are available. Booklets for children and parents, along with a downloadable digital guide, enhance the visitor experience. Souvenirs, books, and educational materials can be obtained from the on-site shop. Restaurants within the premises offer opportunities for refreshments. The museum ensures full accessibility for individuals with disabilities, providing wheelchairs on request.

Location: 86 Quai Perrache, 69002 Lyon, France

Open: Monday–Sunday from 10:30 am to 6:30 pm

Phone: +33 (0) 4 28 38 12 12

2. Museum of Cinema and Miniature
Explore Hyper-Realistic Miniature Exhibits from Iconic Films

The Museum of Cinema and Miniature in Lyon offers an extraordinary experience, showcasing highly detailed replicas from renowned movies such as Robocop, Gremlins, and urban landscapes, all crafted in miniature. Boasting over 1,000 replicated settings, props, artworks, and crafts, the museum delves into the realm of special effects and movie creatures, featuring some full-sized props and costumes.

Georgia Tucker

Situated in the heart of Lyon's historic center, this museum allows you to witness props and costumes from a diverse array of celebrated productions, accompanied by meticulously detailed artwork that demonstrates remarkable precision.

Highlights of the Museum of Cinema and Miniature in Lyon:

- *Miniature Scenery:* Immerse yourself in fully detailed scenes, from medieval alchemical workshops to city alleys, complete with intricate details like jars, steampunk-style machinery, and miniature figures.

- *Micro-Artwork:* Discover exquisite micro-art, including carved matchsticks, eggshells, and tiny origami creations.

- *Film Props and Costumes:* Explore real costumes and props from a wide range of films, including Batman, Stuart Little, Spider-Man, Alien, Hellboy, and more, gaining insights into the special effects of these cinematic masterpieces.

Additional Information: The museum is housed in a 16th-century UNESCO World Heritage building, offering reduced rates for students under 26, the unemployed, and individuals with disabilities. Convenient parking is available at Parkings Saint-Jean and Saint-Georges, and public transportation options include buses and the Metro.

The museum operates on a self-guided tour format, ensuring disability accessibility upon request. To plan your visit strategically, note that peak hours are between 2 pm and 5 pm on weekends, with potential high visitor traffic. The ticket office closes an hour before the museum's closing time.

Location: 60 Rue Saint-Jean, 69005 Lyon, France

Open: Monday–Sunday from 10 am to 6:30 pm

Phone: +33 (0)4 72 00 24 77

3. Lumière Museum
Discover the Birthplace of Cinematography at this Unique Museum

The Lumière Museum in Lyon is a dedicated institution honoring the life and contributions of the Lumière Brothers, pioneers in the world of cinema. Situated at the historical birthplace of cinematography, the museum provides a rich experience through projections, interactive displays, archival documents, artifacts, and insights into the brothers' impactful journey.

For cinephiles, the Lumière Brothers hold a significant place in history, marked by original cameras, advancements in color and 3D photography, and more. At the Musée Lumière, you can explore these milestones and uncover lesser-known aspects of their remarkable legacy.

Georgia Tucker

Highlights of the Lumière Museum in Lyon:

- *Annual Film Festival:* The museum hosts a prominent film festival every October, featuring a festival village with a DVD market, a cinema bookstore, a restaurant, a beer bar, nightly concerts, film exhibitions, and a Lumière Award ceremony.

- *Bookstore and Library:* Explore the on-site bookstore or delve into the library to deepen your understanding of film history. The Café Lumière provides a delightful spot for refreshments.

- *Exhibits:* The museum features three galleries with a mix of permanent and rotating exhibits, offering diverse insights into the Lumière Brothers' contributions.

Additional Information: The museum ensures complete accessibility for individuals with disabilities and provides engaging interactive activities suitable for all ages. Special admission discounts are available for those under 18 or over 60, students, teachers, people with disabilities, and their companions. Children under 7, museum members, and Lyon City Card holders enjoy free entry.

Visitors can opt for a self-guided exploration or enhance their experience with a guided tour at a nominal additional cost. Booking reservations in advance is recommended for guided tours. The multimedia experience integrates tablets, audio guides, and contemporary multimedia tools.

Location: 25 Rue du Premier Film, 69008 Lyon, France

Open: Tuesday–Sunday from 10 am to 6:30 pm (closed on Mondays)

Phone: +33 (0)4 78 78 18 95

4. Musée des Beaux-Arts de Lyon
Embark on a Journey Through Art Across the Ages

The Museum of Fine Arts of Lyon, known as the Musée des Beaux-Arts de Lyon, stands as a municipal treasure showcasing significant art collections spanning from ancient times to contemporary masterpieces. Recognized as one of Europe's premier art museums, it not only regularly features exhibitions by modern artists but also presents works by classical painters, sculptors, graphic artists, and diverse media installations.

Situated within a meticulously restored 17th-century former convent, the museum comprises three distinct buildings: the Abbey, the Palais du Commerce et des Arts, and the Musée des Beaux-Arts.

Key Highlights of Musée des Beaux-Arts de Lyon:

- **The Abbey:** Home to expansive paintings depicting food-related biblical narratives, such as the Multiplication of the Loaves and the Last Supper. This venue is often utilized for gatherings and group events.

- **The Palais:** Primarily housing sculptures from the 19th and 20th centuries, the Palais building contributes to the museum's diverse artistic offerings.

- **Musée des Beaux-Arts:** Serving as the primary repository, this building showcases the museum's extensive collection, tracing the evolution of art and media through various historical periods.

The museum boasts notable works by renowned artists, including Charles Le Brun, Jean-Baptiste Greuze, Renoir, Anet, Cézanne, Van Gogh, Salvator Rosa, Francisco de Zurbaran, Rubens, Rembrandt, Georges Rouault, Henri Matisse, James Pradler, Emile Antoine Bourdelle, and many more.

Georgia Tucker

Additional Insights into Musée des Beaux-Arts de Lyon:

- The museum prioritizes accessibility, providing support for individuals with mobility, hearing, vision, and mental health-related disabilities. Special accommodations can be arranged upon request.

- Holders of the Lyon City Card enjoy access to not only this museum but also numerous other cultural sites and historical landmarks throughout Lyon.

- Amenities on-site include a tea room and restaurant offering picturesque garden views for a tranquil dining experience. The museum store and bookshop provide opportunities to acquire meaningful souvenirs and deepen your understanding of the showcased artworks.

Location: 20 Pl. des Terreaux, 69001 Lyon, France

Opening Hours: Saturday–Monday and Wednesday–Thursday from 10 am to 6 pm, Friday from 10.30 am to 6 pm (Closed on Tuesdays)

Contact: +33 (0)4 72 10 17 40

Official Website: https://www.mba-lyon.fr/en

5. Museum of Contemporary Art, Lyon
Experience Unconventional and Modern Art

The Lyon Museum of Contemporary Art is a captivating venue showcasing artwork created directly on-site by various artists. The exhibits change approximately twice a year, consistently offering a glimpse into the innovative creations of contemporary artists.

It's important to note that the museum may be closed for about six months between exhibits to ensure the seamless preparation of upcoming displays. Located on the northern edge of Parc de la Tête d'Or and south of Grand Casino de Lyon Le Pharaon, this museum provides a dynamic space to explore modern artistic expressions.

Location: Cité Internationale, 81 Quai Charles de Gaulle, 69006 Lyon, France

Phone: +33 (0)4 72 69 17 17

6. History Center of the Resistance and Deportation
Uncover the Stories of French Resistance Heroes

The History Center of the Resistance and Deportation delves into the history of the French Resistance during the Nazi occupation and sheds light on the tragic events of Jewish deportation. Housed in a former French military health school, which the Nazis occupied in 1943, the museum provides a poignant look into this significant period.

As you explore the exhibits, you'll encounter detailed accounts of historical events, including the challenges faced by resistance member Jean Moulin. Conveniently located in Jean-Macé, a short distance southwest of Parc Bechevelin, this museum offers a profound journey into the resilience and sacrifices of those who resisted oppression.

Location: 14 Av. Berthelot, 69007 Lyon, France

Open: Wednesday–Sunday from 10 am to 6 pm (closed Monday–Tuesday)

Phone: +33 (0)4 72 73 99 00

7. Tony Garnier Urban Museum
Discover Urban Art in Tony Garnier's Housing Project

The Tony Garnier Urban Museum is an assemblage of vibrant murals adorning the structures within a housing project envisioned by Tony Garnier. A diverse array of artists contributed to the creation of 24 murals along the exteriors of the buildings.

As an open-air museum, it operates continuously, allowing you to appreciate the murals irrespective of weather conditions. Situated along the northwestern periphery of Les États-Unis on the east side of the city, this urban art haven invites exploration.

Location: 4 Rue des Serpollières, 69008 Lyon, France

Open: 24/7 Phone: +33 (0)4 78 75 16 75

8. Museum of Printing and Graphic Communication
Immerse Yourself in the Evolution of Printing

The Museum of Printing and Graphic Communication provides a fascinating journey into the history of printing, tracing its origins from the Renaissance. Displaying artifacts spanning various epochs, from the inception of printing to the technological advances of the Industrial Revolution, and delving into modern-day photography and graphic design.

Given Lyon's significant role in the printing legacy, the museum not only explores global influences but also contributes to the city's identity. Located in Cordeliers - Jacobins just north of the Cordeliers Metro Station, it offers a comprehensive understanding of the evolution of printing.

Location: 13 Rue de la Poulaillerie, 69002 Lyon, France

Open: Wednesday–Sunday from 10.30 am to 6 pm (closed Monday–Tuesday)

Phone: +33 (0)4 78 37 65 98

9. La Maison des Canuts
Experience Silk Making and Weaving Heritage

Georgia Tucker

La Maison des Canuts is a combined museum and workshop dedicated to Lyon's rich legacy of silk production and artistic weaving. The museum not only showcases exquisite samples of silk craftsmanship but also provides live demonstrations.

While delving into the historical narrative of textiles, the museum also offers insights into the contemporary 21st-century industry, showcasing the latest technological advancements. Situated in Croix-Rousse Est et Rhône, less than a mile northeast of the Croix-Rousse Metro Station, it offers a comprehensive exploration of Lyon's silk heritage.

Location: 10 Rue d'Ivry, 69004 Lyon, France

Open: Tuesday–Friday from 10 am to 1 pm and 2 pm to 6 pm, Saturday from 10 am to 6 pm (closed Sunday–Monday)

Phone: +33 (0)4 78 28 62 04

10. Museum of Puppet Arts
Unveil the World of Puppets

The Museum of Puppet Arts, or Musée des Arts de la Marionnette, is a captivating institution dedicated to puppetry arts. Offering an interactive experience, it stands out as an excellent choice for visitors, especially those with children.

Beyond an impressive display of puppets, the museum provides insights into the mechanics of puppetry, allowing visitors to witness the mastery behind making these figures come to life. Located in Vieux Lyon, a short distance south of the Lyon Saint Paul train station, it promises a delightful exploration of the enchanting world of puppetry.

Location: 1 Pl. du Petit Collège, 69005 Lyon, France

Open: Wednesday–Sunday from 10.30 am to 6 pm (closed Monday–Tuesday)

Phone: +33 (0)4 78 42 03 61

Georgia Tucker

BEACHES NEAR LYON: WHERE TO GO FOR SUN, SAND, AND SURF

Lyon is a sought-after destination for travelers in France, offering a mix of museums, cultural sites, shopping, and exceptional cuisine. Beyond the city's attractions, many are unaware that serene sandy beaches are within easy reach. For those seeking tranquility during their Lyon visit, these beach destinations provide an ideal opportunity to unwind and enjoy leisurely moments.

While exploring the sandy beach options outlined in this guide, consider incorporating luggage storage in Lyon into your plans. Entrusting your belongings to Bounce ensures a carefree experience on the golden sands, allowing you to fully immerse yourself in swimming and leisure activities.

1. L'île de Porquerolles

This sandy beach haven is situated on an island, offering a delightful setting for golden sands and water sports. The island features numerous smaller beaches, providing diverse options for beachgoers. Seafood restaurants, shopping, and horseback riding along the shore add to the island's allure.

Travel Distance from Lyon: Accessible via a six-hour train journey from Lyon Perrache or a comparable drive.

Activity Recommendations: Embark on the Tour Fondue ferry to reach this scenic sandy spot. Whether indulging in water sports with rented gear or simply relaxing under an umbrella, locals frequent this haven for its pristine beaches. Explore the charming communities scattered around the island, creating an opportunity for a delightful journey from one area to another. The ferry ride itself is a memorable experience, offering a unique sense of detachment on an island. Extend your stay with various lodging options available on the island.

2. Argelès-sur-Mer

Situated near the Spanish border, Argelès-sur-Mer boasts one of the finest beaches in proximity to Lyon. The sandy beach offers a vibrant atmosphere with a promenade featuring ample shopping opportunities, swimming spots, and areas for relaxation. Popular among both locals and tourists, the beach tends to be bustling, especially during July and August.

Travel Distance from Lyon: Approximately a five-hour drive or a six-hour train journey from Lyon.

Activity Recommendations: Argelès Beach captivates visitors with its turquoise waters, soft golden sand, and amenities such as sun lounger rentals. Beyond beach activities, explore horseback riding, leisurely strolls along the shore, and opportunities for shopping and fine dining. The beach's proximity to other gems like Collioure and Sain Cyprién allows for easy beach hopping, facilitated by nearby train stations. Despite the distance, the array of attractions makes it a worthwhile destination.

3. Tony Bertrand Swimming Pool

If your schedule doesn't allow for a visit to the golden sands and turquoise waters during your stay in Lyon, you can still indulge in the experience of an impressive outdoor pool. Depending on your location in the city, this local hotspot may be conveniently within walking distance. Alternatively, a short drive or a brief ride on public transportation ensures swift access to this enticing attraction.

Tony Bertrand Swimming Pool Travel Distance from Lyon: Situated within the city limits, reaching this enjoyable pool area takes less than ten minutes by car or a convenient twenty-minute train ride.

Activity Recommendations: While not a beach locale, this exceptional swimming pool within city bounds provides an excellent option for relaxation. Swim, unwind on the pool deck, or partake in swimming classes and water aerobics. Its proximity to various accommodations in the city makes it a practical choice, particularly for families with children.

While Lyon may lack nearby true beaches, the availability of a high-quality pool destination like this ensures a splendid day of swimming, sunbathing, and socializing with friends. For those who appreciate a day at the pool as much as a day at the beach, this offers a delightful alternative.

4. Valras Plage

Renowned as one of the most picturesque beaches near Lyon, Valras Plage boasts ample sandy shores and inviting turquoise waters. Easily accessible to all, visitors can engage in swimming, sunbathing, or the rental of water sports equipment. The shallow waters cater to the enjoyment of little ones along the shore, and a local market provides fresh fish, food, and homemade goods.

Valras Plage Travel Distance from Lyon: Approximately a four-hour drive from the city; reachable in three and a half hours by train from Lyon Part Dieu Station.

Activity Recommendations: Valras Plage epitomizes the classic beach experience, offering golden sands, local eateries, and food trucks for a delightful day in the sun. Consider renting an umbrella and chairs for a comfortable beachside lounge, especially during warm summer days. The beach's proximity to restaurants and shopping enhances the overall experience, making it an excellent choice for either a weekend getaway or a day trip.

Georgia Tucker

CHAPTER FIVE: ACCOMMODATION

CHOOSING WHERE TO STAY IN LYON

If you're planning your first visit to Lyon and wondering about the best areas to stay, whether for a night out, family vacation, or a romantic getaway, you're in the right place. This guide will help you discover the ideal neighborhoods, featuring a comprehensive map and video, along with recommendations for hotels suitable for various budgets and insights into the safest places in Lyon.

Lyon Overview: Situated in the Auvergne-Rhône-Alpes region, Lyon, also known as the Capital of Lights, stands as the third-largest city and the second-largest urban area in France. Rich in history dating back to Roman times, Lyon offers a wealth of historical and cultural experiences, catering to diverse preferences of visitors.

Where to Stay for First-Timers: For newcomers and tourists, the top areas in Lyon include La Presqu'île, Vieux Lyon, Fourvière, Confluence, and Perrache. These neighborhoods are renowned for their popularity, safety, and a plethora of attractions. *La Presqu'île:* Positioned as the best overall arrondissement for first-time visitors, La Presqu'île's central location provides easy access to major attractions like Place des Terreaux, Hôtel de Ville, and Musee des Beaux Arts. This area offers proximity to numerous sights, restaurants, bars, and shops.

Other Notable Neighborhoods:

- *Vieux Lyon:* The historic old town, perfect for those keen on exploring Lyon's rich history with numerous historical attractions.

- *Fourvière:* Home to an unparalleled collection of Roman ruins, setting it apart as a distinctive area in the city.

- **La Croix Rousse:** Provides a unique insight into Lyon's silk merchant history.

Considerations for Different Tastes:

- **Perrache or Confluence:** Ideal choices for budget travelers or those seeking newer, up-and-coming neighborhoods.

Duration Recommendation: If you're wondering how long to stay in Lyon, a long weekend of around three days is recommended for your first trip. This duration allows ample time to explore top tourist attractions and savor a diverse range of traditional Lyonnais dishes.

Recommended Accommodations:

- *Best Area for First-Timers:* La Presqu'île

- *Best Luxury Hotel:* Hotel Le Royal Lyon – MGallery

- *Best Mid-Range Hotel:* Mercure Lyon Centre Beaux-Arts

- *Best Budget Hotel:* Hôtel Vaubecour

Your stay in Lyon promises not just a visit but an immersive experience, blending history, culture, and the vibrant atmosphere of this captivating city.

Map of areas and neighborhoods in Lyon:

When it comes to choosing the right neighborhood to stay in Lyon, I've outlined the eight best areas for tourists and those exploring Lyon for the first time. Each area has its unique offerings, and I'll guide you through what makes them special and why they might be the perfect fit for you.

Best Areas in Lyon for Tourists & First-Timers:

1. La Presqu'Ile

La Presqu'île stands out as the optimal area for first-time travelers, thanks to its central location and excellent transportation links.

Georgia Tucker

Situated at the heart of the city, this UNESCO World Heritage site offers a vibrant mix of top attractions, upscale shopping, pedestrian-friendly streets, and diverse accommodation options. Extending from the base of Croix Rousse hill to the confluence of Rhone and Saone rivers, La Presqu'île is framed by Perrache station and Confluence to the south and Pentes de la Croix-Rousse to the north. Encompassing the 1st and 2nd arrondissements, along with parts of the 4th and the city hall, it's a dynamic district with various facets. The 1st arrondissement is a nightlife hub housing landmarks like Hôtel de Ville, Place de la Comédie, and Opera Nouvel. On the other hand, the 2nd arrondissement is a bustling commercial and shopping area, home to Lyon-Perrache station and Place Bellecour. Brimming with cafes, restaurants, department stores, luxury boutiques, cultural institutions, banks, and government buildings, La Presqu'île caters to both business travelers and those seeking a leisurely vacation filled with culture and relaxation. Notable attractions span from the northern Place des Terreaux to the southern Place Bellecour. At the heart of Place des Terreaux is the 19th-century Fountain de Bartholdi, designed by Auguste Bartholdi, the mind behind the Statue of Liberty. It serves as a popular meeting point surrounded by bars and restaurants. In the 2nd district, Place Bellecour, Europe's largest pedestrian square, serves as a central point connecting four major streets:

- Rue de la République, the primary shopping street leading to Hôtel de Ville and the Opera.

- Rue Victor Hugo and Rue du Plat, guiding you to Perrache.

- Rue du Président Édouard Herriot, lined with luxury shops, leading to the Place des Terreaux.

In the heart of Lyon, along the banks of the Rhone River, the Hôtel Dieu Hospital showcases historical surgical instruments and pharmacy items, providing a glimpse into the medical practices of the past. Constructed in the 12th century and later renovated in the 17th century, this site preserves the evolution of healthcare through the ages.

This area boasts numerous iconic and historical landmarks, with the prominent Church of St Nizier standing out. Originally built in the 6th century, the church underwent finalization in the 16th century, marked by the completion of towering spires that dominate the city skyline.

Within the 1st arrondissement, the Hôtel de Ville, Lyon's 17th-century city hall, graces the landscape between two captivating squares, Place des Terreaux and Place de la Comédie.

In close proximity, Lyon's Opera House, the Opera Nouvel, bears the architectural signature of Jean Nouvel, who redesigned the structure. While the facade and foyer retain their original charm, a distinctive steel and glass barrel-shaped roof was added. Adjacent to this, the Saint Pierre Palace, erected in the 17th century as a royal Benedictine abbey, now houses the Museum of Fine Arts and features a public garden adorned with works by renowned sculptors.

This district is adorned with historic theaters, museums, and cultural centers, interconnected by charming, historic streets. La Presqu'île stands out as a comprehensive destination, seamlessly blending historical and cultural richness with modern tourist amenities and business facilities.

Accommodation options in La Presqu'île cater to all budgets, ranging from backpacker hostels to luxurious hotels. Choose La Presqu'île if you are a first-time tourist seeking historical immersion, wish to explore a diverse array of shops, bars, and restaurants, are on a business trip, or want to visit some of Lyon's most iconic landmarks.

Best places to stay in Lyon in La Presqu'Ile for first-timers:
Luxury ($$$): Hotel Le Royal Lyon – MGallery is a 5-star family-friendly hotel, offering a premium experience for those exploring Lyon for the first time. Centrally located in Lyon, right next to Bellecour station, it is within a convenient walking distance from Old Town, the Fine Arts Museum, and Perrache. The hotel's prime location is complemented by its proximity to the shopping district and a variety of cafes and restaurants.

Mid-Range ($$): Mercure Lyon Centre Beaux-Arts is a popular 4-star hotel situated in Lyon City Center. Perfect for first-time visitors, it provides easy access to key attractions such as Bellecour Square, Lyon's old town, and Bellecour Station. Additionally, it is surrounded by a plethora of charming bars and restaurants, enhancing the overall experience.

Budget ($): Hôtel Vaubecour, a fantastic 2-star hotel, stands out as one of the best budget-friendly options in Lyon. Located in the heart of Lyon on the 2nd floor of the building, accessible via a lift, this hotel offers family rooms and is just a few steps away from Lyon Perrache Train Station. An economical yet comfortable choice for those on a budget.

2. Vieux Lyon (Old Town)

Vieux Lyon, the Old Town quarter of the city, is situated in the 5th arrondissement on the west bank of the Saône river. It constitutes Lyon's most expansive medieval and Renaissance district, ranking among the largest in all of Europe. Vieux Lyon is divided into three parishes: Saint-Paul in the northern Old Town, Saint-Jean in the Old Town center, and Saint-Georges in the southern Old Town.

This district stands out as the premier area for lodging in Lyon, especially for sightseeing, given its wealth of medieval and Renaissance structures, museums, and churches. Notably, it was the initial location in France safeguarded by the Malraux law, dedicated to preserving the country's cultural sites, and is a designated UNESCO world heritage site.

Renowned for its impressive array of churches and cathedrals, reflecting the city's profound religious history, key landmarks include the Cathedral of Saint-Jean, Saint Paul Church, and St Georges Church, each serving as the focal point for their respective parishes. Rue St Jean, starting at St-Jean Cathedral, holds historical significance, hosting events such as the royal wedding mass between Henri IV and Marie de Médicis in 1600.

At the end of Rue St Jean lies the Loge du Change, previously Lyon's stock exchange, transformed into a Protestant place of worship known as the Temple du Change. Branching from the square, Rue Lainerie and Rue Juiverie lead to the St Paul subdistrict.

Ascending by foot or taking the funicular to the summit of Fourvière hill reveals historic attractions and remnants of the Roman city, including the iconic Basilica Notre Dame de Fourvière, Gier Aqueducts, Gallo-Roman Amphitheaters, and Roman bathhouses. The area offers delightful cafes and traditional restaurants, providing ample opportunities to savor local cuisine.

Georgia Tucker

Vieux Lyon boasts numerous museums, such as the Lyon Historical Museum, Gadagne Museums showcasing the Renaissance era and the city's puppetry art, the Movies and Miniature Museum, and the Museum of Gallo-Roman Civilization.

The district is adorned with historic buildings, charming narrow cobbled streets, silk shops, local food specialties, vintage stores, and unique souvenir shops, ensuring a captivating experience that will be remembered for years. Frequently visited by tourists for its rich history and cultural offerings, guest houses and boutique hotels are often housed in medieval buildings with stunning Gothic architecture, allowing visitors to fully immerse themselves in the local culture. Stay in the Old Town if you are interested in history and culture, enjoy museums, appreciate traditional architecture, or prefer accommodations in a hotel built in the Middle Ages.

Best Places to stay in Lyon in Old Town for first-time visitors:
Luxury ($$$): Cour des Loges Lyon, a member of Radisson Individuals, is a 5-star hotel located within walking distance from Saint-Jean-Baptiste Cathedral. It features a swimming pool, rooftop garden, valet parking, sauna, hammam, and an onsite Michelin-starred restaurant, Les Loges. Additionally, it offers a bistro, Café-Epicerie, and La Petite Loge, where guests can partake in cooking classes, wine tasting, and private dinners with the chef.

Mid-range ($$): MiHotel Tour Rose, a family-friendly accommodation conveniently situated in the 5th arrondissement, provides air-conditioned rooms with amenities such as a wardrobe, kettle, microwave, fridge, safety deposit box, flat-screen TV, and a private bathroom.

Budget ($): La Loge Du Vieux Lyon, an excellent bed and breakfast option for a budget stay in the heart of Lyon, offers self-catering accommodation in a historical building. The apartment is equipped with a flat-screen TV and a fully-equipped kitchen.

3. Fourvière

Fourvière is a district situated just west of the old town, positioned on a hill that rises from the River Saone. Originally settled as the Roman town of Lugdunum in 43 B.C., it boasts an extensive collection of Roman ruins, including baths, a theatre, and an Odeon, providing a unique glimpse into a different facet of the city's history.

Hosting the Nuits de Fourvière festival annually from June 1 to July 30, the Roman theatre becomes a spectacular venue, offering a truly special experience for fortunate visitors during these times.

The Gallo-Roman Museum of Lyon-Fourvière, or Lugdunum, serves as a repository of the area's legacy. Housed in a building designed by Bernard Zehrfuss and inaugurated in 1975, the museum delves into the rich Roman history of the region.

Beyond its Roman allure, Fourvière is renowned for La Tour Metallique (The Metallic Tower), an iconic structure designed to rival the Eiffel Tower. With a style reminiscent of its famous counterpart but standing taller at its summit, this tower crowns the highest point in Lyon due to its hilltop location.

Atop the "hill that prays" stands the Basilica of Notre-Dame de Fourvière, exhibiting Romanesque, Gothic, and Byzantine architecture. Built between 1872 and 1884, the basilica is dedicated to the Virgin Mary, credited with saving Lyon from the Black Death. The Festival of Lights, celebrated annually on December 8, pays homage to the Virgin for this historic intervention.

To enhance your experience, it's advisable to ascend via the funicular railway and descend on foot, allowing you to appreciate the scenery

Georgia Tucker

with less strain on your legs. Fourvière is an integral part of the city's UNESCO world heritage site, offering a diverse and thrilling destination for tourists.

Fourvière provides more affordable accommodation options compared to Vieux Lyon. Visitors can choose from various accommodations, including guest houses and apart-hotels. Stay in Fourvière if you are intrigued by Lyon's Roman history, wish to witness a structure challenging the Eiffel Tower, plan to attend the Festival of Lights, or seek to ride on the world's oldest funicular railways.

Best Places to stay in Lyon in Fourvière for the first time:
Luxury ($$$): Villa Maïa, a 5-star hotel situated on Fourvière Hill in Lyon, offers panoramic views of the city. With amenities like an indoor heated swimming pool, a hot tub, a steam room, and a fitness room, guests can also dine at the nearby Michelin-starred restaurant Têtedoie.

Mid-range ($$): Fourvière Hôtel, a popular 4-star family-friendly hotel, is located on Fourvière Hill above Lyon Old Town. The onsite Restaurant Les Téléphones serves bistronomic cuisine with views of the cloisters. Guests can enjoy drinks at Le KFE or venture through the traboule passageway to savor wine at Les Collections.

Budget ($): Le Jardin de Beauvoir, a charming B&B in Old Lyon set in a 19th-century house, is surrounded by a flowered garden with an orchard. Featuring soundproofed family rooms equipped with a coffee machine and a private bathroom with free toiletries and a hairdryer, it offers a delightful and budget-friendly stay.

4. La Croix Rousse

La Croix Rousse is a hill standing over 250 meters tall, earning its name, "the red cross," from a reddish-brown stone cross erected in the 16th century. This neighborhood is divided into two distinct regions: Pentes de la Croix-Rousse, or the slopes, in the 1st arrondissement, and the hill's peak, Le Plateau, in the 4th arrondissement.

Known as "the hill that works" (la colline qui travaille) in contrast to Fourvière and its nickname "the hill that prays" (la colline qui prie), La Croix Rousse underwent significant development in the 18th century. The relocation of silk workshops and the Canuts (silk workers) from the city center shaped the district, resulting in buildings reflecting the signs of this industry.

The tall structures, featuring large vaulted ceilings and exposed wooden rafters, were originally designed to accommodate silk looms. Traboules, covered walkways facilitating the transport of silk between buildings while shielding it from the rain, are prevalent in the district.

In recent years, La Croix Rousse has evolved into a bohemian and culturally vibrant area. It's an ideal choice for those seeking a blend of unique history, breathtaking views, and diverse entertainment options. In the Les Pentes bohemian district, Rue Sainte Catherine and Croix-Paquet boast bars, clubs, cafes, and music venues. For a vibrant restaurant scene, explore Rue Royale in the east and Rue de la Martinière in the west. The Village des Créateurs and Montée de la Grande-Côte offer artist shops and boutiques.

Known as the City of Murals, Lyon showcases painted murals in the trompe-l'oeil style (trick the eye). La Croix Rousse, with the famous Mur des Canuts, is a haven for art lovers. History enthusiasts can explore the Maison des Canuts museum to delve into the silk industry's past. The Amphithéâtre des Trois Gaules, the oldest

Georgia Tucker

Roman Amphitheatre of Gaul, and the statue of Joseph Marie Jacquard, inventor of the Jacquard Loom, can also be found in the neighborhood.

To reach La Croix Rousse, take the funicular to the top and walk down to the center, relishing panoramic views of the city. Accommodations in Pentes de la Croix-Rousse are primarily guesthouses, offering a more affordable option than the city center.

Choose La Croix Rousse if you are fascinated by the history of the city's silk workers, appreciate a thriving cultural scene, seek stunning views, or wish to visit the site of one of France's first worker uprisings.

Best Places to stay in Lyon in La Croix Rousse:
Budget ($): Hotel Saint Vincent, a 3-star budget-friendly hotel within walking distance of restaurants, bars, and attractions like the Lyon National Opera and Lyon's Museum of Fine Arts. Offering newspapers, luggage storage, and a 24-hour front desk.

Mid-range ($$): Hôtel Lyon Métropole, a 4-star hotel located on the Saone River, providing a tranquil experience. Easily accessible by Bus number 40 and close to a public bike rental station and Cuire Metro Station, offering direct access to the city center.

5. Confluence

Confluence, situated in the 2nd arrondissement, derives its name from the confluence of the Rhone and Saone rivers. Historically an industrial hub with factories, prisons, and the city's main port, Confluence underwent a significant transformation and urbanization in the late 20th century.

The area, once dominated by vehicles transporting industrial materials, now showcases striking new buildings, designed by renowned global architects. Well-connected by public transport, Confluence benefits from Perrache train station, offering direct links to Part-Dieu Station and St-Exupéry Airport through Rhône-Express trams.

A standout example is the Musee des Confluences, a remarkable Deconstructivist building resembling a floating cloud of steel and glass, paying homage to the region's industrial past. The museum focuses on nature, science, anthropology, and arts and crafts.

A walking tour of Confluence includes visits to Musée des Confluences Lyon, unique structures like Orange Cube and Euro News Building, the Shopping Center Pôle de Commerces et de Loisirs de Confluence, Pont des Arts, and various riverfront housing complexes.

Beyond its attractions, Confluence's development along the river has introduced shops, restaurants, hotels, homes, and offices. The area boasts a vibrant nightlife, with numerous bars along the river Saône, especially around Marché Gare and Le Sucre, known for prominent music venues and clubs.

This revitalization has attracted tourists, locals, and new residents, injecting vitality into what was once a dull, uninviting part of the city. Opt for Confluence if you plan to visit the Musee Des Confluences, appreciate beautiful river views, or seek accommodation in a newer, emerging neighborhood.

Best Places to Stay in Lyon in Confluence:

Budget ($): MOB HOTEL Lyon Confluence, a 3-star family-friendly hotel within walking distance of Musée des Confluences, Musée des Confluences Tram Stop, and a shopping center. Features a terrace, on-site restaurant, and an Italian organic self-service canteen.

Mid-range ($$): Aparthotel Adagio Lyon Patio Confluence, a 4-star accommodation with family rooms in Lyon's 2nd arrondissement. It's a short walk from Lyon-Perrache Train Station and Perrache Metro Station, offering easy access to Sainte-Blandine Tram Stop, Confluence shopping center, and Confluences Museum.

Mid-range ($$): Novotel Lyon Confluence, a 4-star hotel in the center of Lyon on the banks of the Saône River. Close to the Vaporetto Station, the A6 and A7 motorways, Confluence Commercial Centre, and Lyon Perrache Train Station.

6. Perrache

The district of Perrache is situated in the 2nd arrondissement, south of Le Presqu'ile and upstream of Confluence, nestled between the Rhone and the Saone. Historically overlooked, it has acquired the moniker "derriere les voutes," translating to "behind the vaults."

In recent years, Perrache has undergone substantial redevelopment efforts, receiving investments aimed at modernizing the area to attract both residents and tourists. Consequently, it now offers accommodation at highly affordable rates, making it an excellent choice for budget-conscious travelers.

Adding to its appeal is the presence of the Lyon-Perrache train, tram, and metro station. While it may no longer hold the title of the largest and busiest station in Lyon, it remains a bustling and popular transportation hub. This means visitors can benefit from the cost-effectiveness of the area while enjoying quick and convenient access to more renowned parts of the city.

Choose Perrache if you are on a budget and seeking economical accommodation, traveling by train, or interested in staying in an emerging neighborhood.

Best Places to Stay in Lyon in Perrache for First-Timers:

Mid-range ($$): Aparthotel Adagio Lyon Patio Confluence, an excellent 4-star hotel located in Lyon's 2nd arrondissement. A short walk from Sainte-Blandine Tram Stop, Lyon-Perrache Train Station, and Perrache Metro Station. Features family rooms, a cold sweet and savory buffet breakfast, and a laundry room with a washing machine, a tumble dryer, and ironing facilities.

Budget ($): MEININGER Hotel Lyon Centre Berthelot, providing good value accommodation in Lyon. A short walk from Musée de la

Resistance, offering a bar, private parking, a shared lounge, and a terrace.

Budget ($): ibis Lyon Centre Perrache, a 3-star family-friendly hotel and one of the best choices for budget-conscious travelers. Located in Lyon city center, within a 5-minute walk from Place Bellecour. Perrache train station, bus, and tram stops are a convenient 2-minute walk away.

7. Brotteaux

Les Brotteaux, situated in the 6th arrondissement between the Rhone River and the city's primary railway track, is also known as the Morand quarter. Its urbanization traces back to the late 18th century, led by the renowned architect Jean-Antoine Morand Jouffrey, whose distinct style is evident in many of the area's buildings.

Key landmarks include the Gare Des Brotteaux, an old railway station no longer in service since 1983, the Palais De Flore, and the Boulevard Des Belges. For enthusiasts, the Parking Morand serves as a dedicated site to Morand Jouffrey's life and works. The quarter boasts buildings and mansions with a 1930s Art Deco style, adding diversity to its architectural landscape.

Apart from its historical architecture, Les Brotteaux is celebrated as one of Lyon's culinary hubs. From traditional bouchons serving typical Lyonnais cuisine to European delights, the area hosts a plethora of renowned restaurants. Le Splendid, owned by esteemed chef Georges Blanc, and La Brasserie Des Brotteaux, dedicated to honoring Lyon's culinary traditions, are among the notable establishments.

Within walking distance from Gare de Lyon-Part-Dieu, Les Halles Paul Bocuse, named after master chef Paul Bocuse, offers an indoor food market showcasing the best of Lyonnaise Cuisine. The quarter is also home to Michelin-starred places like the modern Peruvian Miraflores and the traditional Pierre Orsi.

Beyond its culinary offerings, families can enjoy the expansive Parc de la Tête d'Or, France's largest urban park, featuring a zoo, boating lake, botanical gardens, miniature railway, and various recreational trails.

Choose Brotteaux if you wish to dine in some of the city's finest restaurants, appreciate the legacy of Jean-Antoine Morand Jouffrey, and experience Lyon's rich culinary traditions.

Best Places to Stay in Lyon in Brotteaux:
Budget ($): Ibis Budget Lyon Centre – Gare Part Dieu, a 2-star budget-friendly hotel in the central 3rd district, within an easy walk from Part-Dieu Train Station, offering soundproofed guest rooms with a flat-screen TV.

Mid-range ($$): Mercure Lyon Centre – Gare Part Dieu, a 4-star family-friendly hotel in Lyon's business district, a short walk from

Gare de Part-Dieu TGV Train station and Gare Part-Dieu-Vivier Merle Metro Station, providing easy access to Lyon's Old Town. The Rhone Express Tramway stops with links to Lyon-Saint-Exupéry Airport are also conveniently nearby.

Mid-range ($$): Warwick Reine Astrid – Lyon, a 4-star kid-friendly hotel located opposite Tête d'Or Park, close to the Cité Internationale and the city centre. A 10-minute walk from Massena metro station facilitates exploration of Lyon.

8. Guillotiere

Guillotiere, situated on the east bank of the Rhône, spanning both the 7th and 3rd arrondissements, is an ideal choice for those seeking a lively nightlife and a multicultural atmosphere. This neighborhood, characterized by its youthful and student-centric vibe, boasts a plethora of trendy bars, clubs, and concert venues.

Renowned for its diverse mix of people from various social and ethnic backgrounds, Guillotiere offers attractions that cater to a broad range of visitors. History enthusiasts can explore landmarks like the 15th-century Castle Of La Motte, the exquisite 19th-century Notre-Dame Saint Louis church, and the intriguing Cemeteries Of La

Guillotiere, each holding captivating secrets within their beautiful exteriors.

For those interested in World War II history, the Centre d'Histoire de la Résistance et de la Déportation (CHRD) provides insight into the French Resistance. Outdoor enthusiasts can enjoy walking and cycling along the Berges du Rhône, next to the river, or take a refreshing dip in the attractive outdoor pools with slides and fountains at the Piscine du Rhône. Culinary enthusiasts can explore the unique shops and restaurants in Chinatown.

A visit to the Musée & Institut Lumière offers a glimpse into the history of cinema, where the Lumière brothers invented the Cinématographe and created the first film in 1895.

Guillotiere's transportation hub ensures convenient travel, and the array of shops and traditional dining options cater to various preferences. Described as a melting pot of history, culture, and entertainment, Guillotiere is an excellent choice for those who wish to experience a diverse range of offerings in Lyon.

Stay in Guillotiere if you seek accommodation in a culturally and ethnically diverse location, want to explore the Chinatown area, and desire a well-rounded experience of Lyon.

Best Places to Stay in Lyon in Guillotière:
Budget ($): Mama Shelter Lyon, a 3-star hotel in the 7th arrondissement, within walking distance from Jean-Macé Metro Station, providing direct access to Stade de Gerland and Lyon-Part-Dieu Train Station. Family rooms and a 24-hour front desk are available.

Georgia Tucker

Budget ($): Résidence Ôtelia Affaires & Bien-être, a budget-friendly accommodation near T2 Route de Vienne tram stop and T4 Jet d'Eau – Mendès France tram stop, offering rooms with a kitchenette.

Luxury ($$$): InterContinental Lyon – Hotel Dieu, an IHG hotel, a 5-star establishment located in the 2nd arrondissement, close to the Museum of Fine Arts of Lyon, Fourviere Roman Theatre, and Part-Dieu Train Station.

BEST HOTELS IN LYON

Selecting accommodation in Lyon requires careful consideration. Staying in the heart of Vieux Lyon is convenient for exploring the city's UNESCO-classified sites, but be mindful of potential challenges like high prices and some street noise. Alternatively, Fourvière Hill offers more space and panoramic city views, accessible by a steep uphill walk or Funicular railway. In the 2nd arrondissement, just across the Bonaparte Bridge from Vieux Lyon, sought-after hotels overlook elegant squares such as Place Bellecour and Place des Célestins. The Presqu'île area along the River Rhône, spanning the 1st and 2nd districts, features new luxury hotels. If you're seeking a hipster vibe, the La Croix Rousse area to the north offers affordable accommodation. Lyon currently boasts a range of hotel options, making it an excellent time to plan your stay.

Top Backpacker Hotels in Lyon: Lyon's modern hostels have evolved beyond their basic predecessors. These backpacker hotels now feature stencil art, designer furnishings, and offer healthy cuisine. Among the favorites are Slo Living Hostel at 5 rue Bonnefoi (tel. 04-78-59-06-90) in Saxe Gambetta, providing four or six-bed dormitories as well as private double rooms; Away Hostel at 21 rue Alsace Lorraine (tel. 04-78-98-53-20) on the slopes of Croix-Paquet in the 1st district, offering dorms for four to eight occupants and private doubles with Nespresso coffee machines; and Ho36 Hostel at

36 rue Montesquieu (tel. 04-37-70-17-03) in Guillotière, featuring mixed and women-only dormitories (in Lyon Opéra only) along with private family rooms and doubles.

Your Expert Guide to Lyon's Top 26 Hotels

Lyon stands out as one of France's most captivating cities, offering travelers a plethora of cultural attractions, delectable local cuisine, and breathtaking scenery. Whether you desire luxury or budget-friendly options, there's a hotel to cater to every traveler's preferences. As a tour operator organizing wine tastings in the city, I've gathered insights into my guests' hotel experiences, creating an updated list of the best hotels for those visiting Lyon. Read on for the latest recommendations! Regardless of your budget or preferred amenities, this list will streamline your search, making it easier to find the ideal place to stay in Lyon. Discover more about the best hotels in Lyon for 2024 and beyond.

Choosing Accommodation as a Traveler in Lyon

Locals affectionately refer to Lyon as "human-sized," emphasizing its walkability. For an optimal experience, I recommend staying in the city center and as close to the rivers as possible. While public transportation is excellent, being in the heart of the action is advantageous for tourists. Stay within the outlined area or as close to it as possible. Lyon is defined by two converging rivers at the city's base (known as the Confluence), and it is dominated by two prominent hills. This geographical aspect is crucial when selecting accommodation, considering your mobility and preferences to avoid staying on the two significant hills.

Lyon's Top Luxury Hotels

Georgia Tucker

Intercontinental at Grand Hôtel-Dieu

The Intercontinental Hôtel-Dieu stands out as my top recommendation for Lyon visitors. Ideally positioned along the Rhone River, it provides stunning views of either the river or the grand courtyard. Its central location makes it a perfect hub for exploring the entire city. Housed in a historic building, the Intercontinental features an impressive cocktail bar beneath a magnificent architectural dome, offering the city's finest hotel breakfast.

Location: 2nd Arrondissement, Prime spot along the Rhône

Price: High-end (€€€)

Villa Maïa

For the epitome of luxury, look no further than Villa Maïa. Catering to those with a taste for exquisite detail and discretion, this establishment is situated near the ancient Roman amphitheater with a breathtaking spa. Affiliated with the renowned Michelin Starred Têtedoi restaurant, owned by Lyon magnate Christophe Gruy, Villa Maïa is an opulent member of the Leading Hotels of the World network.

Location: 5th Arrondissement, Fourvière Hill

Price: Ultra-luxury (€€€€)

Villa Florentine

A member of the Relais & Châteaux group, Villa Florentine offers a captivating view above the Old Town. Lavish rooms, a gastronomic restaurant with an exceptional terrace, and a must-try summer poolside experience characterize this establishment. Newly introduced apartment suites provide additional space and privacy for a truly indulgent stay.

Location: 5th Arrondissement, just above the Old Town

Price: Ultra-luxury (€€€€)

Boscolo Hotel

Centrally located along the Rhône river in a splendid Haussmann era building, the Boscolo Hotel is synonymous with sleek luxury and opulent detail. This Italian Boscolo hotel group member features an underground spa with a swimming pool, inviting guests to enjoy Thalasso massages under an ancient vaulted ceiling.

Location: 2nd Arrondissement, on the Rhône river in the center of town

Price: Ultra-luxury (€€€)

Cour des Loges - Currently Closed for Renovation

Cour des Loges, a renowned 5-star hotel situated in the old town, is temporarily closed for essential renovations. A fixture in the historic area, the hotel has been undergoing improvements to enhance its allure. The last time I had a glimpse inside in 2018, it seemed a bit worn but full of character, reminiscent of Moulin Rouge meets a nautical theme. This fabulous location in a beautiful building is expected to reopen with substantial improvements in November 2023.

Georgia Tucker

Top Boutique Hotels in Lyon, France

Lyon offers a delightful array of charming boutique hotels, each with its own local touch.

Hotel de l'Abbaye Named after the adjacent medieval Abbey, this charming new hotel is located in a serene part of town, just across from the Abbey. Central yet tucked away for privacy, it boasts a handful of rooms and a sophisticated restaurant named l'Artichaut.

Location: 2nd Arrondissement, in the quiet neighborhood of Ainay

Price: Moderate to High (€€€)

Hotel le Phénix

Recently renovated and exuding modern charm, Le Phenix is ideally situated along the Saône River in the Old Town. With a quaint bar and an impressive breakfast spread, it offers affordability and a helpful concierge team. Part of a local independent group, it shares resources with three hotels, ensuring excellent recommendations.

Location: 5th Arrondissement, on the Quai de Saône in Vieux Lyon, near Elody's Pub

Price: Moderate to High (€€-€€€)

MiHotel Lyon

Embracing a unique concept with digital check-ins and scattered suites across prime city locations, MiHotel offers a variety of beautifully presented rooms. With no lobbies or restaurants, the focus is on providing a hassle-free experience with large and beautifully decorated suites.

Location: Various prime spots throughout the city

Price: Moderate (€€)

Lyon's Premier Hotels for Business Travelers

Lyon, a hub for international business, caters to business travelers with top-notch accommodations.

Marriott Cité International

Perfectly situated for business endeavors at the Centre de Congrès, Marriott Cité International offers spacious rooms and a business-friendly atmosphere. Located in a modern complex wrapping around the northwestern edge of Parc de la Tête d'Or, it provides convenient access for corporate activities.

Location: 6th Arrondissement, inside the Cité International including the Centre de Congrès

Price: Moderate (€€)

Warwick Reine Astrid

Discover an oasis in Lyon at the Warwick Reine Astrid Hotel – a true marvel! Offering a more upscale experience than the Marriott, it is located on the opposite side of Parc de la Tête d'Or along the exquisite Boulevard des Belges, adorned with magnificent mansions. The Reine Astrid is a luxurious establishment, meticulously appointed, and features a delightful garden – a rare gem in Lyon.

Location: 6th Arrondissement, nestled among bourgeois mansions on the southern edge of the park

Price: High (€€€)

Georgia Tucker

Radisson Blu Lyon

Despite its exterior resembling a brown crayon, the Radisson Blu is a standard hotel with a fantastic city view from its restaurant. Situated near the Part-Dieu train station – a bustling area perpetually under construction – it offers convenient access to transportation hubs and Les Halles de Paul Bocuse.

Location: 3rd Arrondissement, in proximity to the Part-Dieu train station

Price: Moderate to High (€€-€€€)

Moxy Lyon

The recently inaugurated Moxy Hotel is conveniently located within the St Exupéry Airport. Boasting a vibrant atmosphere and stylish design, it's an excellent choice for those with late arrivals or early departures.

Location: Inside St Exupéry Airport

Price: Moderate (€€)

Chic and Contemporary Hotels in Lyon

For the discerning traveler seeking design-oriented accommodations, Lyon offers a selection of the best.

Mama Shelter Lyon

Mama Shelter Lyon exudes style with its trendy designer rooms, a noteworthy restaurant featuring brunch, and a cool rooftop bar. Located in Lyon's 7th Arrondissement, slightly off the tourist path, it is surrounded by a plethora of vibrant bars and restaurants.

Location: 7th Arrondissement, a hub of stylish activity

Price: Moderate (€€)

Okko Hotels Lyon

Strategically positioned along the Rhône river, Okko Hotels Lyon is known for its chic interiors. Housed in a stunning Haussmann-era building, it offers a modern and design-oriented ambiance. Many satisfied clients have praised its prime location and contemporary design.

Location: 6th Arrondissement, on Quai de Rhône, near river boats

Price: Moderate (€€)

Maison Nô

Nestled in the heart of Presqu'Île, Maison Nô is a well-located hotel boasting a chic rooftop bar. With amenities like a gym, sauna, and private lobby, this stylish establishment occupies a former bank building.

Location: 2nd Arrondissement, in the vibrant downtown area

Price: High (€€€)

Charming Hotel Silky by HappyCulture
Exterior view of Hotel Silky by HappyCulture

Hotel Silky has garnered positive reviews for its intimate ambiance and central location. Nestled in the heart of the 2nd Arrondissement, this small yet delightful hotel boasts vibrant and lively interiors, complemented by spacious rooms and well-appointed bathrooms.

Georgia Tucker

The friendly staff ensures a pleasant stay, offering a satisfying breakfast experience.

Location: 2nd Arrondissement, situated in the center of town amidst excellent shopping and dining options.

Price: Moderate (€€)

Lyon's Top Classic French Hotels

For those seeking a more classical atmosphere, Lyon offers a selection of favored traditional hotels.

Hotel Carlton

Centrally Located Carlton Hotel This expansive hotel, housed in a splendid Haussmann-era building in the heart of Presqu'Île, features a captivating old-world charm. Guests can enjoy the unique experience of the ancient and elegant cage elevator. The hotel also offers a hammam and spa for added relaxation.

Location: 2nd Arrondissement, right in the midst of the bustling city center.

Price: High (€€€)

Le Royal
Exquisite Fabrics at Le Royal Hotel in Lyon With a delightful vintage ambiance, Le Royal, a 5-star hotel, exudes charm with its colorful French country fabrics. Linked to the Institut Paul Bocuse cooking school, guests have the opportunity to savor dishes prepared by France's future culinary talents.

Location: 2nd Arrondissement, situated on the central Place Bellecour.

Price: High (€€€)

Globe et Cecil

Chic Room at Globe et Cecil Hotel Part of a local hotel group, Globe et Cecil, along with Le Phénix, offers 59 individually decorated rooms steeped in charm. The hotel, located in the historic 2nd Arrondissement, near the charming Place des Jacobins, also features a restaurant serving a fabulous breakfast.

Location: 2nd Arrondissement, in proximity to the delightful Place des Jacobins.

Price: Moderate to High (€€-€€€)

Hotel Mercure Beaux Arts

Elegant Grand Hotel Mercure Beaux Arts A classic choice, Hotel Mercure Beaux Arts, known for its well-appointed rooms, enjoys an ideal location. While the design may reflect a 2003 aesthetic, the hotel's prime position near the beautiful Places des Jacobins, adorned with an elegant fountain, compensates for any outdated decor.

Location: 2nd Arrondissement, near Places des Jacobins.

Price: High (€€€)

Georgia Tucker

Best Budget Hotels in Lyon

While the term "budget hotel" may seem rare, some affordable gems still exist. Here are recommendations for excellent accommodations in Lyon for under €150 per night.

Hotel Taggat

Taggat Hotel in the 6th Arrondissement Situated in the upscale 6th Arrondissement, Hotel Taggat offers an affordable option that doubles as an art gallery. Guests can even purchase the artwork featured in their rooms. Located in the tranquil Foch neighborhood, just across the river from the Opéra, it provides a peaceful escape from the city buzz.

Location: 6th Arrondissement in the Foch neighborhood, across the river from the Opéra.

Price: Budget-friendly (€)

Hotel Edmond W.

Lovely Courtyard at Hotel Edmond W. Receiving commendations from satisfied patrons, Hotel Edmond W. is a boutique hotel situated in the sophisticated Brotteaux neighborhood. Conveniently close to the train station without the chaos of ongoing construction, the hotel features a charming garden and a delightful breakfast.

Location: 6th Arrondissement, in Brotteaux, a refined neighborhood near the Part-Dieu station.

Price: Budget-friendly (€)

Pilo Hotel

Stylish and Contemporary Pilo Hotel Image: Chic industrial restaurant at the Pilo Hotel

Pilo Hotel is a recent addition to Lyon, housed in a spacious industrial building featuring sleek, modern design. Functioning as both a hotel and hostel, it offers a unique combination of amenities, including a restaurant and co-working space. Situated in the Les Pentes neighborhood, accessibility involves navigating stairs. The hotel boasts a cool, minimalist design, creating a welcoming atmosphere with a trendy vibe.

Location: 1st Arrondissement, adjacent to a captivating abandoned Roman Amphitheatre that often goes unnoticed by tourists.

Price: Affordable (€)

Georgia Tucker

CHAPTER SIX: SHOP LIKE A LOCAL

BEST MARKETS IN LYON

Lyon, being one of France's largest and most vibrant cities, hosts a diverse array of markets that provide an enriching shopping experience, distinct from conventional malls. These markets cater to various preferences, ensuring a culturally immersive shopping venture for everyone. Explore the top 10 markets in Lyon.

1. Les Halles de Lyon

Discover Gourmet Delights Les Halles de Lyon stands out as an iconic indoor food market renowned for its exceptional gourmet offerings. Housing 48 vendors, it showcases a range of produce, ingredients, and fully prepared meals. Beyond food, you can find an assortment of beverages, including fine wines and spirits, as well as chocolates and sweets. Located just south of Aire De Jeux Garibaldi, approximately 1.5 miles east of Lyon's city centre.

Location: 102 Cr Lafayette, 69003 Lyon, France

Operating Hours: Monday–Saturday from 7 am to 7 pm, Sunday from 7 am to 1 pm

Phone: +33 (0)4 78 62 39 33

2. St Antoine Market

Experience a Vast Outdoor Food Market St Antoine Market, positioned along the banks of the Soane, is a sprawling outdoor food market offering a diverse selection of regional and imported produce. Specialties like pizza and spit-roasted chickens, along with international dishes from Asia and North Africa, contribute to the market's variety. Explore this market on the east side of the Saone, just **northeast of Pont Bonaparte.**

Location: 11 Quai des Célestins, 69002 Lyon, France

Operating Hours: Tuesday–Sunday from 6 am to 1 pm (closed on Mondays)

3. La Croix Rousse Market

Explore a Market in an Historic Working-Class Neighborhood La Croix Rousse Market, situated in an old working-class neighborhood, offers a diverse array of food from local vendors. Traditional and organic produce is available, with a dedicated section for organic products. Additionally, every Tuesday, a market featuring manufactured goods such as clothing, shoes, fabrics, and tools is held. Located just an 8-minute drive northwest of Lyon's city centre.

Location: Bd de la Croix-Rousse, 69004 Lyon, France

Operating Hours: Tuesday and Friday–Sunday from 6 am to 1.30 pm, Wednesday–Thursday from 6 am to 1 pm (closed on Mondays)

4. Les Puces du Canal
Explore a Expansive Flea Market

Les Puces du Canal stands as a well-liked flea market with a multitude of permanent and visiting merchants offering an extensive array of items. Housing 200 permanent merchants and 400 unpackers, ensure to allocate sufficient time to explore the vast offerings.

Beyond the myriad of items, this flea market boasts 7 restaurants within its premises, eliminating the need to venture elsewhere for a meal. Located in the Villeurbanne neighborhood, approximately 15 minutes by car from the heart of Lyon.

Location: 5 Rue Eugène Pottier, 69100 Villeurbanne, France

Operating Hours: Thursday and Saturday from 7 am to 1 pm, Sunday from 7 am to 3 pm (closed Monday–Wednesday and Friday)

Phone: +33 (0)4 69 85 66 28

5. Marché aux Bouquinistes
Experience a Charming Book Market

Marché aux Bouquinistes, a popular book market, offers a diverse selection of books set up along a picturesque riverbank in Old Lyon. The variety available is substantial, including a wide array of kids' books in multiple languages.

Affordability is a notable aspect of this market, making books here more budget-friendly compared to traditional bookstores. Explore this market along the eastern bank of the Saone, just west of the Jardin du Palais St Pierre.

Location: 9 Quai de la Pêcherie, 69001 Lyon, France

6. Montchat Castle Market
Delight in a Quaint Flower Market

Montchat Castle Market, a small venue primarily focused on flowers, also offers an assortment of other goods, including food items. With around 40 traders in total, the market features pastries, wine, and various produce.

Similar to other markets in the city, Montchat Castle Market presents a diverse selection of produce, cheeses, meat, and prepared dishes. Explore this charming market in northeastern Montchat, just a few steps from Square de l'Eglise.

Location: Pl. du Château, 69003 Lyon, France

Operating Hours: Wednesday and Saturday from 6 am to 1.30 pm (closed Sunday–Tuesday and Thursday–Friday)

7. Marché de la Tête d'Or

Enjoy a Market Amid Lush Surroundings

Marché de la Tête d'Or is a delightful market set within the park of the same name, offering an array of food and flowers for sale.

Vendors provide typical French fare alongside international offerings.

A common and enjoyable way to experience this market is to gather food and other items for a picnic in the park surrounded by vibrant greenery. Located in the Brotteaux neighborhood, approximately a mile and a half east of the city centre.

Location: 77-89 Rue Tête d'Or, 69006 Lyon, France

Operating Hours: Wednesday and Saturday from 6 am to 1.30 pm (closed Sunday–Tuesday and Thursday–Friday)

8. Marché de Monplaisir
Discover a Range of Organic Foods

Marché de Monplaisir is renowned for its diverse selection of organic foods, easily accessible via multiple public transport points. The offerings extend beyond traditional French fare, encompassing a wide variety of organic foods.

Within this market, you'll encounter a substantial array of Asian and Italian options, representing some of the finest culinary selections in the area. Located in northeastern Monplaisir, just a few steps away from the Monplaisir - Lumière Metro Station, across from the museum.

Location: Pl. Ambroise Courtois, 69008 Lyon, France

Operating Hours: Tuesday, Thursday, and Saturday from 6 am to 1.30 pm, Wednesday from 1 pm to 7 pm (closed Sunday–Monday and Friday)

9. Marché Alimentaire Victor Augagneur
Experience a Quaint Riverside Market

Marché Alimentaire Victor Augagneur is a narrow and densely packed riverside market offering fresh food beyond standard French fare. A notable feature is the selection of Levantine food, featuring Middle Eastern and Lebanese ingredients and dishes.

Primarily offering various meats, the market also presents abundant fruit, cheese, olives, and wine. Situated on the east side of the Rhone in Préfecture, north of the Guillotière - Gabriel Péri Metro station.

Location: Quai Victor Augagneur, 69003 Lyon, France

Operating Hours: Thursday from 6 am to 12.30 pm and 2 pm to 8 pm, Saturday–Sunday from 6 am to 1.30 pm (closed Monday–Wednesday and Friday)

Phone: +33 (0)4 72 10 30 30

10. Jean Macé Market
Explore a Dynamic City Hub

Jean Macé Market is a lively produce market featuring an array of goods, including clothes, records, books, and more. Located in the famous district of the same name, it is easily accessible by various modes of transportation.

Vendors at this market are known for their knowledge about the products, making it an ideal place to inquire about sourcing and even growing some produce yourself. Situated near the Jean Macé Metro Station and Lyon-Jean-Mace train station.

Location: Pl. Jean Macé, 69007 Lyon, France

Georgia Tucker

Operating Hours: Saturday and Wednesday from 6 am to 1.30 pm (closed Thursday–Friday and Sunday–Tuesday)

Phone: +33 (0)4 72 10 30 30

SHOPPING IN LYON

Shopping hours vary across Lyon's districts. In Vieux Lyon, shops are often open on Sundays but closed on Mondays (and sometimes Tuesdays and Wednesdays in low season). Meanwhile, in the 2nd district, the norm is more traditional, with Monday or Tuesday to Saturday openings and closures during lunchtime and on Sundays.

Vieux Lyon boasts art galleries and unique boutiques. Boulangerie du Palais, located at 8 rue du Palais (tel. 04-78-37-09-43), is a popular bakery known for its delightful tartes au praline. Antic Wine, situated at 18 rue du Boeuf (tel. 04-78-37-08-96), is a captivating and top-rated wine shop in France.

In the 1st district on Place Sathonay, the new travel-inspired shop Hyppairs (tel. 06-67-54-20-82) combines clothing, home décor, and a cozy cafe. The 2nd district's wide avenues focus on designer and high-street brands, with concentrations of retail shops north of place Bellecour. Rue des Archers, our favorite shopping street, features chic Parisian clothing brands and renowned chocolate shops like Bouillet at no. 14 (www.chocolatier-bouillet.com; tel. 04-78-42-98-40) and Bernard Dufoux at no. 15 (www.chocolatsdufoux.com; tel. 04-72-77-57-95).

The historic Passage de L'Argue, linking rue du Président Edouard Herriot with rue de la République, houses established merchants of hats, umbrellas, knives, and shaving brushes. The largest shopping center in Lyon, Centre Commercial La Part-Dieu at 17 rue du Dr. Bouchut in the 3rd district (www.centrecommercial-partdieu.com; tel. 04-72-60-60-62), boasts over 235 boutiques.

Browsing the Markets

Sunday morning (8 am to 1 pm) is an ideal time for shopping in Vieux Lyon, coinciding with the Marché de la Création on Quai Romain Rolland, featuring over 150 artists showcasing jewelry, ceramics, and sculptures.

For organic food, visit Marché de la Croix-Rousse at boulevard de la Croix-Rousse (Tues, Fri, and weekends 6 am–1:30 pm) and Marché du Soir Place Ambroise Courtois (Wed 2 pm–8 pm) near Lumière Museum in the 3rd district. For flowers and food, explore Marché Victor Augagneur on Quai Victor Augagneur (Fri–Sun 6 am–1:30 pm; Thurs 2 pm–8 pm) and Place Carnot (Sun 6 am-1:30 pm) in the 2nd district.

Best Workshop-boutiques

Discover workshop-boutiques showcasing Lyon's silk industry across the city. A notable choice is L'Atelier de Soierie at 33 rue Romarin (www.atelierdesoierie.com; tel. 04-72-07-97-83), where traditional Lyonnais techniques are employed to print silk carrés. Don't miss Brochier's sister boutique, at the foot of the Tour Rose on rue du Boeuf in Vieux Lyon (May to November), showcasing silkworm metamorphosis from hatching to cocoon spinning and transformation into moths (subject to mulberry leaf availability).

Key areas

Rue du Président Herriot, adorned with its graceful 19th-century structures, creates an ideal backdrop for luxury boutiques. Discover fine antiques and vintage books on rue Auguste Comte or at La Cité des Antiquaires, 117 boulevard Stalingrad in Villeurbanne. Lyon takes pride in hosting one of the world's premier chocolate factories:

Georgia Tucker

Bernachon at 42 cours Franklin Roosevelt. Bouillet, situated at 15 place de la Croix Rousse and 14 rue des Archers, astounds with its exquisite 'ganaches of chocolate' and renowned macaroons.

Markets
Les Puces du Canal, Lyon's historic flea market (Sundays 6:00-13:00), is situated on the outskirts at 1 rue du Canal in Villeurbanne. To delve into why Lyon is a gourmet's haven, explore its food markets on quai St-Antoine or boulevard de la Croix-Rousse (Tuesday to Sunday mornings).

SHOPPING TIPS IN LYON

Shopping Centers
The Presqu'île area houses major department stores like Printemps. For casual shopping, Lyon's Part-Dieu shopping centre at 17 rue du Docteur Bouchut is ideal and ranks among Europe's largest, featuring over 230 stores, including the renowned Galeries Lafayette. Confluence hosts Lyon's newest and most glamorous megamall, also known as Le Centre Confluence. Accessible by tram with ample parking.

Opening Hours
Most shops typically operate from Monday to Saturday between 09:30 and 19:00 (with closures between 12:00 and 14:00) and are closed on Sundays. Some small grocery stores open on Sunday mornings.

Souvenirs

Rue Saint Jean in Vieux Lyon is the go-to place for selecting thoughtful souvenirs for loved ones. It offers a variety of items, including leather goods, furniture, jewelry, Lyonnais silk, and fabrics. Delight in exploring delis offering sausages, tinned confit duck legs, bottles of Burgundy, and jars of foie gras.

Tax Information

VAT (Value Added Tax) ranges from 5% to 19.6%, depending on the purchased goods. A tax-free shopping scheme is available for non-European Union citizens. To qualify, spend over €175 on the same day in the same store and obtain a valid customs stamp upon final departure from the EU. Look for the Tax Free Shopping sticker in shop windows.

Georgia Tucker

CHAPTER SEVEN: EAT LIKE A LOCAL

LOCAL FOODS YOU HAVE TO TRY IN LYON

8. Cervelle de canut
SPREAD

Cervelle de Canut is a fresh cream cheese spread originating from Lyon, France. This delectable spread is seasoned with vinegar, salt, pepper, olive oil, garlic, and fresh herbs. Despite its name, "silk weaver's brains," it is entirely vegetarian. The dish earned its unique title from the silk weavers (canuts) of Lyon in the 19th century. Due to financial constraints, the weavers devised this spread, often enjoyed on bread or potatoes.

7. Coussin de Lyon
Dessert

Georgia Tucker

Invented in 1960 by chocolatier Voisin, Coussin de Lyon is a sweet treat shaped like a soft pillow. The name refers to the silk cushion placed under a 7-kilo candle and a gold écu coin offered to the Virgin Mary during the 1643 plague epidemic in Lyon. This green candy features almond paste and chocolate ganache subtly flavored with liqueur. A cherished dessert in Lyon, Coussin de Lyon also makes for an ideal gift.

6. Tablier de Sapeur
Offal Dish

Tablier de Sapeur is a traditional dish from Lyon, France. Made with beef tripe, white wine, garlic, onions, lemon juice, mustard, olive oil, eggs, salt, pepper, and breadcrumbs, it offers a unique culinary experience. The tripe is marinated, coated in breadcrumbs, and fried until tender. Typically served with boiled potatoes and sauce gribiche, this dish showcases Lyon's culinary heritage.

5. Poires au Vin
Dessert

Poires au Vin, a renowned French dessert, hails from the Beaujolais wine-growing region. Featuring pears, red wine (often Beaujolais), and flavorful ingredients like honey, sugar, cinnamon, vanilla, orange zest, peppercorns, and cloves, this dessert is a sensory delight. The pears are poached, and the resulting sauce, infused with rich flavors, is drizzled over the slightly firm, poached pears.

4. Saucisson Brioche
Sausage Dish

Saucisson Brioche, a specialty of Lyon, involves baking a whole sausage, usually coated in pistachios, inside a brioche loaf. This dish combines a substantial sausage with brioche dough that is less sweet and egg-rich than typical breakfast brioche. Baked until golden brown, it is served warm in slices, making it a delightful pairing with a glass of Beaujolais.

3. Lyon-Style Sautéed Calf's Liver
Offal Dish

Lyon-style sautéed calf's liver is a classic representation of Lyonnaise cuisine, emphasizing the use of authentic local ingredients prepared through traditional cooking methods. The dish features sautéed and caramelized onions paired with succulent calf's liver. Prepared with generous amounts of butter, the dish is traditionally deglazed with vinegar, imparting acidity to complement the sweetness of the onions and the robust flavor of the liver. Lyon-style liver is then elegantly presented, garnished with chopped parsley, and served alongside roasted or mashed potatoes.

2. Lyonnaise Salad
Salad

Originating from Lyon, the Lyonnaise Salad is a beloved dish featuring lettuce, bacon, croutons, and a poached egg atop. It stands as a hallmark of Lyonnaise cuisine, dating back to the 1500s when Catherine de Medici instructed her chefs to craft innovative dishes using ingredients from across France. Today, this salad is a staple on the menus of quaint French bistros known as bouchons, specializing in comforting, regional fare.

1. Rosette de Lyon
Sausage/Salami

Rosette de Lyon, a French sausage with origins in Lyon, derives its name from the city. Crafted from a blend of pork meat, sea salt, peppercorns, and garlic encased in natural beef casing, this rich and flavorful sausage undergoes a month-long curing process, resulting in sweet and mellow flavors. The term "rosette" is thought to allude to its rose-colored appearance. Best enjoyed sliced, it pairs excellently with baguettes and cheeses such as Grana Padano or Taleggio.

BEST RESTAURANTS IN LYON

Lyon, recognized globally for its culinary excellence, proudly holds the title of the gastronomic capital of France. This southeastern city is a haven for food enthusiasts, featuring an extensive array of delectable local ingredients and a roster of esteemed chefs, contributing to its own Michelin star galaxy.

In a city where gastronomy is a way of life, the competition among exceptional eateries is formidable. Even the most discerning food connoisseurs will find the plethora of outstanding dining options challenging to navigate. However, we have embraced this challenge and curated a selection of the finest establishments—ranging from local to international, catering to various budgets—epitomizing the culinary essence of Lyon, France.

Fun Fact: Lyon boasts one of the highest concentrations of Michelin stars per capita globally. The city is brimming with fine-dining establishments offering locally sourced produce and tantalizing tasting menus for both lunch and dinner, reaffirming its status as the gastronomic hub of France!

Best Restaurants in Lyon for Local Cuisine

Lyon holds a distinct advantage when it comes to the best restaurants, being a treasure trove of premium French ingredients. Noteworthy mentions include meats, especially saucissons, prominently featured on lunch menus, alongside locally cultivated fresh produce. The city, situated on the doorstep of Burgundy, also takes pride in its exceptional cheese and wine offerings.

In this section highlighting Lyon's best restaurants, we've carefully selected three establishments offering the pinnacle of local cuisine, ranging from must-try fine dining to affordable, yet delightful, experiences at a renowned Lyonnais institution.

1. L'Auberge du Pont de Collonges/Paul Bocuse

A local culinary icon, Paul Bocuse has indelibly shaped Lyonnais cooking, making his name synonymous with Lyon's food culture. Inaugurated in 1956 in collaboration with his father, the eponymous restaurant earned its first Michelin star in 1958, a number that quickly multiplied to three by 1965. Bocuse retained the prestigious triple-Michelin star status until 2020.

On the menu:

- Black truffle soup with a pie topping (crafted for President Giscard d'Estaing in 1975)

- Sea bass en croûte (a visual delight with exquisite pastry)

- Lobster and zander quenelle in champagne sauce

Price: Set menus commence at €185 per person, with mains priced at €80.

Fun Fact: Lyon serves as a captivating stop on Saone-Rhone river cruises—explore the enticing itineraries for a memorable journey.

2. La Mère Brazier

Established in 1921, La Mère Brazier has been a stalwart advocate for local cuisine since its modest inception. Eugénie Brazier's delectable creations quickly won the hearts of the city's most discerning palates, elevating La Mère Brazier to an institution in Lyon cherished by both culinary enthusiasts and locals. Since assuming leadership in 2008, Chef Mathieu Viannay has preserved the establishment's art déco design, solidifying its culinary prowess.

On the menu:

- Poularde de Bresse, seasonally prepared

- House artichokes with foie gras

- Restaurant's interpretation of saucisson

- Noteworthy cheese board

- Madagascar vanilla soufflé paired with Sauternes ice cream

Price: Set menus commence at €80 per person, with mains priced at €65.

Georgia Tucker

3. Le Musée

Nestled on a quiet side street (Rue des Forces) opposite Saint-Nizier church, Le Musée offers a wallet-friendly and vibrant dining experience, staying true to the hearty traditions of Lyon cuisine. The unpretentious yet delightful atmosphere features shared tables adorned with red and white checked tablecloths, accompanied by service that comes with a welcoming smile.

On the Menu:

- Andouillette (tripe sausage)

- Quenelles de brochet (fish dumplings)

- Various robust Lyonnais recipes with pork

Price: Anticipate spending around €30 for lunch.

Did you know? Lyon isn't just about glorious food; the city also offers a plethora of attractions. Explore our guide to the best Lyon has to offer.

Best Lyon Restaurants for Fusion Cuisine

As the gastronomic hub of France, Lyon seamlessly executes fusion cuisine, whether blending foreign and French flavors or infusing local culinary techniques with international influences.

1. Les Apothicaires

A delightful fusion of French and Brazilian influences awaits at Les Apothicaires, housed in a charming restaurant resembling an antique shop. The kitchen, led by French Ludovic and Brazilian Tabata, harmoniously crafts plant-based and smoked dishes with

Scandinavian and South American nuances, earning Les Apothicaires a Michelin star.

On the Menu:

- Seasonal ingredients take center stage, resulting in weekly changes for lunch and monthly alterations for dinner.

- Starters feature pulses and vegetables, while mains showcase the fish or meat of the day.

- Unique sides, such as fish paired with coffee and smoked coconut mousse.

Price: Lunch menus start at €43, and dinner at €77.

2. La Sommelière

La Sommelière, led by Japanese sommelière Shuko Hasegawa and chef Takafumi Kikuchi, stands as a beacon of exceptional modern French dining in the heart of old Lyon. Despite its intimate setting, the restaurant has earned a coveted Michelin star, with its renowned menu reflecting a harmonious fusion of culinary expertise. The establishment's popularity is evident in its substantial waiting list for reservations.

On the Menu:

- Seasonally curated dishes by Chef Takafumi, with the tasting menu evolving monthly.

- Highlights include the 'fish of the day, selected according to the chef's imagination,' game options, and an inspired cheese board.

- A curated list of Japanese or Scottish whiskies serves as a fitting conclusion to the meal.

Price: The tasting menu is priced at €82.

Did you know? The Rhone Valley boasts chateaux that rival those in the Loire. Explore the reasons why [here](link to Rhone Valley article).

3. Takao Takano

Chef Takao, honing his culinary skills at the base of Mount Fuji, brings his reverence for simple delights to Lyon, earning two Michelin stars for his eponymous restaurant. With a commitment to cherishing and elevating produce, Takao Takano offers one of the best-value lunches in town.

On the Menu:

- Simple seasonal ingredients transformed into sublime dishes.

- The lunch tasting menu aptly named 'desire.'

Price: Lunch is priced at €50, while dinner menu options start at €110.

4. La Bijouterie

In a culinary feat, La Bijouterie seamlessly combines Asian flavors with local Lyon ingredients, creating a standout dining experience. Each meal unfolds as a journey of discovery, featuring Asian classics like kimchi and miso paired with regional staples such as mustard and pork cuts.

On the Menu:

- Starters may include scallops and mussels with lemongrass and cauliflower kimchi.

- Dessert options range from smoked chocolate with trout egg to Katsuobushi.

- A extensive wine list offers a diverse selection of foreign and French wines.

Price: The dinner menu is priced at €74.

Best Restaurants in Lyon for Other Types of Cuisine
While Lyon is renowned for its robust traditional fare, the culinary capital of France also excels in diverse cuisine options. This section highlights some outstanding eateries that offer a delightful departure from the usual sausages and veal.

1. Culina Hortus
For those seeking vegetarian or pork-free dining, Culina Hortus, translating to "kitchen garden" in Latin, provides an elevated gourmet experience. Positioned not only as a Lyon gem but also a pioneer in plant-based dining across France, the restaurant sources ingredients nationwide, including the country's sole quinoa production.

On the Menu:

- Seasonal creations featuring generous combinations of pulses, grains, fruits, and vegetables.

- Examples include Jerusalem artichokes with cognac or celery polenta paired with celery mayo.

Price: The lunchtime tasting menu is priced at €35, while the dinner version is €70.

Georgia Tucker

Did you know? Explore Lyon's delectable dining scene conveniently on a self-drive boating holiday. Learn more about the possibilities [here](link to self-drive boating holiday).

2. Cercle Rouge

Situated just steps away from the Rhône, Cercle Rouge offers a warm and eclectic atmosphere with a menu that draws inspiration from around the globe. Featuring influences from Asia, Latin America, and even Britain, this welcoming restaurant caters to a diverse palate. The vibrant décor complements its youthful and artsy clientele, making Cercle Rouge one of Lyon's most budget-friendly dining spots.

On the Menu:

- Exotic fusion such as Mexico and France in foie gras tacos.

- Asian influences in teriyaki fish and sashimi.

- A touch of Britain with beef steaks and banoffee pie.

Price: Mains are priced at €13, and a 3-course lunchtime menu is available for €21.

CHAPTER EIGHT

EXPLORING LYON'S BEST EXPERIENCES

Lyon is a city of diverse wonders, offering a mix of historical charm and modern energy. Whether you're captivated by trompe l'oeil murals, seeking treasures at a flea market, or drawn to the enchanting Festival of Lights, Lyon promises an array of delightful experiences. Let's delve into the very best activities this city has to offer.

1. Discover the Post-Industrial Beauty of La Confluence

Venture south of Lyon's city center to witness the captivating urban renewal project, La Confluence. Initiated in 2000, this ambitious project aimed to expand Lyon's city center while prioritizing sustainability. Formerly an industrial wasteland, La Confluence now boasts futuristic structures like Christian de Portzamparc's Hôtel de Région headquarters, Jean Nouvel's Tour Ycone, and Kengo Kuma's Hikari, the world's first positive-energy city block. Don't miss the iconic Musée des Confluences and the vibrant Le Sucre, housed in a former sugar warehouse.

Georgia Tucker

2. Go Big on Brocante At Les Puces Du Canal

Experience the bustling atmosphere of Les Puces du Canal, a renowned flea market along the Jonage Canal in Villeurbanne. Since 1995, this market has been a treasure trove, offering everything from second-hand books and furniture to jewelry and vinyl records. Witness the lively interactions among antique dealers, haggling and enjoying white wine. Bring cash and arrive early, as the market operates on Thursdays and Saturdays from 7 am to 1 pm and on Sundays from 7 am to 3 pm. Additionally, enjoy a showcase of vintage cars every first Saturday of the month.

3. See the City Aglow at Fête Des Lumières

The Fête Des Lumières stands as Lyon's beloved annual spectacle, tracing its origins back to 1852. What began with residents placing candles in windows to celebrate a new Virgin Mary statue has transformed into a grand festival of light and color. Each year, around December 8, Lyon becomes a dazzling dreamscape with streets, parks, squares, and building facades adorned with installations from local and international artists. Immerse yourself in the vibrant energy of this illuminated celebration.

4. Check Out the Street Art at the Peinture Fraîche Festival

Step into the vibrant world of aerosol art at the Peinture Fraîche Festival, a dynamic celebration of street art. This annual festival, held in October, features around fifty graffiti artists from across the globe leaving their mark on Lyon and the Halle Debourg, a transformed freight sorting warehouse. Whether you're admiring giant murals, observing artists in action, or enjoying concerts and performances, this street art extravaganza promises to reshape your perspective on this ever-evolving art form.

5. Watch A Film (Or Twelve) At the Lumière Film Festival

While Paris often takes the spotlight in cinematic history, Lyon is the true birthplace of cinema as we recognize it. The Lumière brothers, pioneers of the Cinématographe, a groundbreaking device for recording, developing, and projecting motion pictures, hailed from Lyon. Their legacy is celebrated at the annual Festival Lumière, spanning eight days in October. With screenings, premieres, and

Georgia Tucker

discussions across 35 cinemas, this festival is a cinephile's delight, offering opportunities to encounter renowned actors and filmmakers.

6. Master the Hills of The Historic Croix-Rousse District

Since the nineteenth century, Lyon's Croix-Rousse district, known as 'the hill that works,' has been synonymous with the city's silk industry. Now a vibrant bohemian area, it proudly preserves its silk-weaving heritage. Explore numerous independent bars, restaurants, galleries, and shops, all while enjoying panoramic views of the city. The district is home to Le Mur des Canuts, Europe's largest mural, a trompe l'oeil depicting its rich history.

7. Visit the Musée Urbain Tony Garnier

Located in the États-Unis district, the Musée Urbain Tony Garnier stands as urban planner Tony Garnier's masterpiece. Redefining workers' housing and enhancing living conditions, this social housing estate underwent regeneration in the 1980s. The district now features 25 murals celebrating Garnier's visionary architecture. The museum offers a weekly guided tour, providing insight into a captivating reproduction of a 1930s-era dwelling.

8. Reboot Your Wardrobe At Lyon's Vintage Boutiques

Lyon, a hub of France's garment history, is renowned for producing exquisite silks for luxury brands. The city's vintage stores, filled with top-quality designer clothing, old movie posters, and unique homewares, are a treasure trove. Explore Elephant Vintage Store on Rue Hippolyte Flandrin for an excellent range of retro sportswear. Additionally, keep an eye out for vintage clothing and furniture fairs at La Sucrière, a warehouse of treasures on the tip of Presqu'Ile.

9. Let loose at Woodstower Festival

Bid farewell to summer at Woodstower, an eco-friendly festival nestled in the picturesque Miribel Jonage Park and nature reserve. Running for five days at the end of August since 1998, the festival seamlessly blends rap and electro genres. Past performances featured NTM, Todd Terje, Paul Kalkbrenner, Nekfeu, and Jeanne Added. Beyond live music, the festival offers theater, a slow-dance stage, a retro-gaming area, and even horse riding. Just forty minutes from Lyon city center, Woodstower's uplifting vibes make it a perfect daily escape.

10. Check Out Contemporary Art at Galerie Slika

Situated on Presqu'Ile, Galerie Slika occupies a former workshop, serving as a dynamic platform for both emerging and established artists since 2014. While emphasizing street art, Slika presents a diverse array of contemporary works spanning various disciplines. Renowned artists such as Parisian visual artist 2Shy, illustrator Jean Jullien, sculptor Steph Cop, and painter Nelio have all exhibited their creations here. With its diverse and vibrant atmosphere, the gallery is a recommended visit, offering not only art but also a pleasant experience, complete with coffee and cookies at its charming counter cafe.

11. Admire the Amphitheater of the Three Gauls

Take a historical journey by sitting on the steps of the Amphitheater of the Three Gauls, transporting yourself back to Roman Gaul. Located at the base of La Croix-Rousse hill, this amphitheater hosted shows and circus games, originating in 19 AD above the old Gallic town of Condate. Expanded by Emperor Hadrian a century later, it reached dimensions of 147 by 120 meters. Beyond entertainment, the amphitheater served as a meeting place for representatives of 60 Gallic nations, engaging in diplomatic matters around the federal altar. Notably, it witnessed the persecution of Sainte-Blandine and Saint Irénée, early Christian martyrs, influencing the region's conversion to Christianity. Discovered in 1834 and excavated in the 1860s, the amphitheater is now closed off but can be observed from its surrounding fences.

12. Wander the Place Bellecour

Place Bellecour, located at Lyon's heart, is not only the largest pedestrian square in Europe but also the third largest square in France. It is a pivotal stop in any Lyon itinerary. Positioned in the central point of the peninsula between the Saône and the Rhône in the 2nd arrondissement, all distances in the city are measured from this square. With two pavilions housing the tourist information office and an art gallery, Lyon's major shopping streets converge here. At the center stands the equestrian statue of Louis XIV, while the square's south features two fountains amid trees, creating a picturesque park. Place Bellecour is a lively hub throughout the day and night, hosting shopping, socializing, and nightlife activities.

13. See the Exhibitions at La Maison de Canuts

La Maison de Canuts, situated on the Croix-Rousse plateau, serves as both a workshop and a museum dedicated to silk craftsmanship. The permanent exhibition traces the origin of silk, explaining the silkworm cycle and detailing the manufacturing process of gold and silver threads. Delve into the history of silk weavers, their impact on Lyon, and the significance of the silk industry in Europe. Exhibits also cover the Lyonnaise fabric organization, the invention of Jacquard, and the Canuts' revolts in 1831 and 1834. The venue showcases generations of silk creations dating back to the 16th century. Experience the Jacquard invention through weaving demonstrations on a handloom, and inquire about additional tours exploring the traboules used by the Canuts.

Address: 10 Rue d'Ivry, 69004 Lyon

14. Try a Salade Lyonnaise at Le Poêlon d'Or

Savor the flavors of authentic Lyonnaise cuisine at Le Poêlon d'Or, a dining establishment dedicated to upholding the culinary traditions passed down by Lyonnaise mothers. The restaurant, committed to quality and tradition, offers a warm ambiance complemented by wooden furnishings in its century-old venue, recognized as a French heritage site. Awarded the "Best Cork Winner" at the 2017 "Gastronomy and Wine Trophy," Le Poêlon d'Or features a family menu that includes affordable lunch combinations of starters, main courses, and desserts starting from 25€. Indulge in a gastronomic journey with options such as Salade Lyonnaise, Cervelle des Canuts with herbs and smoked duck breast, or Gravlax salmon with potato waffles. For the main course, explore Traditional Lyon Quenelle of Pike in two variations – one with crayfish sauce and the other with Bechamel sauce and white mushrooms. The pan-fried veal sweetbread with mashed potatoes, cream, and morel mushrooms is another popular choice. Complete your meal with classic praline pie or Coupe Mont Blanc for dessert.

Address: 29 Rue des Remparts d'Ainay, 69002 Lyon

15. Enjoy a Beaujolais Wine Tasting Half-Day Trip

Embark on a half-day gourmet wine-tasting excursion in Southern Beaujolais, immersing yourself in the highlights of this picturesque region. Discover the history of the area as you stroll through

Georgia Tucker

charming golden stone villages, often likened to Tuscany, with a chance to explore the medieval village of Oingt. This tour offers a unique opportunity to learn about the Beaujolais region while savoring its finest wines, including the Beaujolais Nouveau. Visit family wineries, understand the concept of 'Terroir,' and indulge in a traditional silk worker's breakfast known as a "machon." This engaging half-day tour provides a delightful and educational experience near Lyon. Sample over a dozen wines, ranging from white and rosé to red, accompanied by croissants, cheeses, and other bread.

16. Explore the Presqu'île

Discover the heart of Lyon by exploring Presqu'île, the central part nestled between the Rhône and the Saône Rivers. Stretching from the foot of the Croix-Rousse hill in the north to the convergence of the rivers in the south, this "almost island" encompasses the first and second arrondissements. Uncover the largest pedestrian square in Europe, Place Bellecour, surrounded by commercial streets boasting luxury boutiques, top-notch restaurants, theaters, and cultural venues. Notable landmarks include the Théâtre Des Célestins, a remarkable Baroque building, and the iconic Bartholdi Fountain monument at Place des Terreaux. Further south, explore the Grand Hôtel-Dieu, a stunning neoclassical structure housing shops, accommodations, and vibrant bars, contributing to Lyon's lively nightlife. Journey into the 2nd arrondissement towards Perrache and La Confluence for additional experiences.

17. Visit the Musée des Beaux-Arts

Lyon's Musée des Beaux-Arts stands as one of France's largest art museums, housed within a stunning Renaissance building that originated as a 17th-century Benedictine abbey. Referred to as the

"Little Louvre," this museum is a regional favorite, drawing visitors to its extensive collection of fine art. The impressive array includes works by renowned artists such as Rubens, Véronèse, Rembrandt, Géricault, Poussin, Delacroix, and Gauguin. The museum also showcases statues, artifacts, antiques, and artwork dating from antiquity, featuring pieces from ancient Egypt, including sarcophagi and the gates of Ptolemy, as well as works from the Near East. The ground floor boasts sculptures from the Medieval and Renaissance eras, including stuccos from the old baroque refectory of the abbey. In the municipal garden, 19th-century statues dot the landscape, and collections of coins and medallions add to the cultural richness. The vibrant courtyard at the museum's entrance serves as a popular gathering spot for locals throughout the day.

Address: 20 Pl. des Terreaux, 69001 Lyon

18. Photograph the Opera National de Lyon

The Opera National de Lyon, situated at Place de la Comédie, combines classical architecture with a contemporary flair. Its semi-cylindrical dome, illuminated with red lights at night, adds a distinctive touch to the cityscape. Statues guarding the opera house overlook the square, where a popular Lyon bar, Les Muses, awaits behind them on the seventh floor. Explore the historical interior design of this neo-classical venue through a guided tour, revealing ceiling frescoes featuring classical motifs, golden engravings of flowers, faces, and borders. The opera house hosts a diverse range of performances, including operas, solo acts, chamber concerts, choral performances, and the Lyon Opera Ballet. The schedule is available on the opera house's website, offering a glimpse into the upcoming season. The square outside the opera house often buzzes with locals seated on the steps, creating a lively atmosphere.

Address: 1 Pl. de la Comédie, 69001 Lyon

Georgia Tucker

19. Take Your Family to Walibi Rhône-Alpes Amusement Park

Nestled in the commune of Les Avenières, Walibi Rhône-Alpes stands as the largest theme park in the Rhône-Alpes region, spanning an expansive 35 hectares. Boasting over 33 rides, it's a favored destination for families, especially if tickets are purchased three days in advance for a discounted experience. The park offers a variety of thrilling rides, including Mystic, Timber, Generator, Le Totem, Woodstock Express, Airboat, Le Galion, and Hurricane, appealing to an adult audience. Family-friendly attractions like Gold River, La Coccinelle, Bambooz River, Melody Road, Dock'N Roll, Tiki Academy, and Les Plongeurs de L'Extreme provide shared experiences. Younger children can enjoy Concert'O, Volt-O-Vent, Les P'Tits Chaudrons, Le Petit Vapeur, Balloon Race, Wab Band Tour, and numerous play areas such as Explorer Adventure, Festival City, and Exotic Island. Exciting dining options, including the Jazz Sugar Club and Golden Burger, add to the park's appeal.

Address: 1380 Rte de la Corneille, 38630 Les Avenières Veyrins-Thuellin

20. Rest Your Feet on a Sightseeing Cruise

Partake in a delightful sightseeing cruise in Lyon, offering a wonderful opportunity to witness the city's prominent landmarks and monuments. This 2.5-hour cruise includes a delectable 3-course meal featuring exquisite French cuisine such as duck, dab fillet, poultry tarts, and praline tarts. Immerse yourself in this gourmet experience while receiving informative commentary about Lyon's renowned sights, available in either French or English.

21. Walk the Streets of Vieux Lyon

Nestled between the Fourvière Hill and the Saône River, Vieux Lyon is renowned for its charming Renaissance alleyways and traboules. These historical passageways, once discreet shortcuts allowing locals to navigate without leaving buildings, reveal the city's rich past. Although most traboules are now closed to traffic, you can explore picturesque inner courtyards reflecting the region's former prosperity. Head to Saint-Paul in the north, where historic homes, the upper middle-class district, and the financial center reside. Rue du Bœuf offers Michelin-starred restaurants and designer outlets, showcasing Lyon as the gastronomic capital of France.

22. Visit the Notre Dame de Fourvière Basilica

Situated on the hill of Fourvière, chosen by the Romans in 43 BC, the Notre Dame de Fourvière Basilica is an iconic masterpiece. Construction began in 1872, designed by Pierre Bossan and supervised by Louis Sainte-Marie-Perrin. The basilica, dedicated to the Virgin Mary, features mosaics and motifs depicting her significance to France and Christianity. A golden bronze statue of the Virgin Mary and an angel with a gleaming spear grace the exterior. Inside, stained-glass windows and marble accentuate the ceiling frescoes in rich greens and blues. Take a stroll outside for a breathtaking panoramic view of Lyon.

Address: 8 Pl. de Fourvière, 69005 Lyon

23. Check Out the Traboules of Lyon

Vieux Lyon harbors a network of traboules, and passageways allowing seamless travel from street to street without venturing outdoors. Lyon boasts 400 traboules, each with a unique history, although only 40 remain open today. These passageways, painted in various pastel colors, were crafted to provide efficient shortcuts through Vieux Lyon's intricate streets. Embark on a tour of the Canut workshops and their traboules at Place de la Croix-Rousse or explore the Vieux-Lyon traboules near its metro station. Signs featuring a lion's head or bronze shield guide your path. Discover the longest traboule between 54 Rue Saint-Jean and 27 Rue du Bœuf or opt for an informative tour of these fascinating historical passages.

24. Wander the Musée Lumière

Musée Lumière, or the Institut Lumière, transcends the concept of a film museum. It encompasses a library, family villa, park, factory, and documentation center dedicated to the Lumière brothers' profound contributions to cinematography, photography, and various other inventions. The villa, once home to Antoine Lumière, father of the renowned inventors Auguste and Louis, comprises four levels, each featuring distinct projections and interactive showcases.

During your visit, detailed displays unravel the distinct roles of each brother, their collaborative ingenuity, and the profound impact they had on scientific and historical realms. Louis Lumière is notably credited with inventing the Cinematograph in 1895, with the first film shot in the garden. An additional viewing experience awaits in the garden's "Le Hangar," a mini-cinema. The villa also functions as a photographic plate manufacturing factory, the largest of its kind in Europe.

Address: 25 Rue du Premier Film, 69008 Lyon

25. Visit Cathedral Saint-Jean

Nestled in Vieux Lyon, Cathedral Saint-Jean stands as a captivating monument with three adorned entrances and massive oak doors amidst cobblestone streets. Situated in Lyon's 5th district along the right bank of the Saône River, this cathedral is a harmonious blend of Roman and Gothic styles. Inside, a 16th-century astronomical clock and 12th-century stained-glass windows depicting scenes from the Old and New Testaments add to its allure.

The cathedral's construction spanned over three centuries, from 1175 to 1480, making it a significant symbol of Lyon. Officially named "la primatiale Saint-Jean-Baptiste-et-Saint-Étienne," it reflects Lyon's historical role as the Primate of All the Gauls, holding judicial supremacy over main archbishops in France. The intricate clock within serves both as a perpetual clock and a religious calendar, calculating saints' days and celestial positions above the city.

Address: Pl. Saint-Jean, 69005 Lyon

26. Explore Halles de Lyon Paul Bocuse

Situated in Cordeliers at the heart of the Presqu'ile, Halles de Lyon Paul Bocuse stands as Lyon's inaugural indoor food market. Established in 1859 to honor Lyon's gastronomic dedication, this recently renovated 13,000-square-meter structure hosts over 48 vendors, offering a diverse array of culinary delights and ingredients. Chef Paul Bocuse's association elevates the market's prestige, making it a renowned destination for gastronomic excellence.

Within this market, you'll encounter expertly organized vendors, including La Mère Richard, celebrated for its cheeses, Cave Fac&Spera, renowned for wines and spirits, and Chez Les Gones, an authentic Lyonnaise restaurant. Lyon's reputation as the gastronomic capital of France finds embodiment in the exceptional quality and variety of offerings within this culinary haven.

Address: 102 Cr Lafayette F, 69003 Lyon

Georgia Tucker

27. Relax in Parc de la Tête d'Or

Located in the 6th arrondissement of Northern Lyon, Parc de la Tête d'Or stands as one of France's largest urban parks, spanning over 105 hectares. This expansive green space encompasses four rose gardens, a botanical garden, a velodrome, numerous greenhouses showcasing plants from around the world, an equestrian facility, a mini-golf station, a zoo, a mini-train, and statues scattered throughout its picturesque landscape. Popular among joggers and cyclists, the park's crystal-clear lake offers the opportunity for summer boating.

Parc de la Tête d'Or offers a myriad of activities. Visitors can leisurely stroll around the park, admire the amenities, and appreciate the villas along the entrances. The vast green space invites picnics with various scenic viewpoints, while the playground entertains children with carousels and other rides. Cafes and vendors overlooking the serene lake provide a perfect setting for lunch, snacks, or coffee conversations.

28. Take a Tour of the Cinema and Miniature Museum

Situated in Lyon's Renaissance district, the Cinema and Miniature Museum is a testament to Lyon's pivotal role as the birthplace of cinema. This unique museum showcases special effects and the art of miniatures, making it the sole establishment of its kind in Europe. Its collections emphasize filmmaking techniques predating the digital era.

Within, visitors encounter models ranging from robots, monsters, and mythological characters to historical figure costumes and superhero outfits. Founded by artist Dan Ohlmann, the museum boasts 120 miniature scenes and over 450 film props from iconic movies, illustrating the techniques employed by major film studios. Additionally, visitors can explore Ohlmann's workshop.

Address: 60 Rue Saint-Jean, 69005 Lyon

29. Explore the La Croix Rousse Neighborhood

Renowned as Europe's silk city, Lyon harbors the La Croix-Rousse district, historically home to silk manufacturers. The district's ascending hillside features tiered buildings, embodying the rich heritage of the textile industry and silk workers known as canuts. Strolling through this area unveils Lyon's cultural essence, preserved through stairwells, traboules, and buildings housing weaving looms.

The district's slopes reveal its unique lifestyle, with numerous silk boutiques and workshops located in the eastern part near the Rhône. Bordered by the Rhône and Saône rivers, the plateau houses the main square, Place de la Croix-Rousse. Hosting one of the city's largest and liveliest outdoor food markets, La Croix-Rousse welcomes visitors daily, excluding Mondays.

30. Take a Guided Food Tour in the Old Town

Delve into Lyon's culinary legacy within its oldest district during a comprehensive 4-hour guided food tour. Navigate hidden passages through traboules, uncovering the culinary gems of Vieux Lyon while savoring authentic Lyonnais cuisine. Your local guide will introduce you to culinary artisans, offering insights into their creations and the inspiration behind them. With five distinct tasting stops featuring 14 diverse dishes, this tour serves as a fulfilling equivalent to lunch. Further details and a personal review of the Lyon food tour can be found here.

As you meander through medieval streets, passing notable sites like the Cathedral of Saint Jean, gain knowledge about local cuisine and discover authentic experiences beyond typical tourist areas. Marvel at hidden courtyards within the traboules while enjoying your tastings, and appreciate the terracotta-tiled roofs of the pastel-colored district. The meeting point for the food tour is at the statue of Monseigneur Lavarenne.

31. See the Gallo-Roman Museum of Lyon-Fourvière

Uncover Lyon's Gallo-Roman cultural heritage by visiting Lugdunum on the hills of Fourvière. The concrete theater, seamlessly blending with the natural landscape, is nestled within lush slopes. The Lugdunum museum boasts one of France's finest archaeological collections, spanning from prehistoric times to the era of Christianity. Exhibits showcase the ancient metropolis, including urban layouts, culture, circus games, trade systems, the military, and currencies. Highlights include a walkable Mosaic, the theater, the Coligny calendar, and diverse Celtic treasures.

Address: 17 Rue Cleberg, 69005 Lyon

32. Rejuvenate at Grand Parc Miribel Jonage

Grand Parc Miribel Jonage stands as one of Europe's largest peri-urban natural parks, spanning 2,200 hectares of natural parkland and 3,000 hectares of undeveloped land. With 850 hectares of forests, the park offers hiking and mountain biking circuits, a golf course, and a 350-hectare lake with numerous beaches. The nature reserve hosts over 1,000 species, including 800 plants, 25 mammal species, and 230 bird species. Beyond nature trails, the park offers various sports activities such as climbing, trampolining, mountain biking, rollerblading, tennis, table tennis, badminton, golf, and archery. Additionally, enjoy water activities at Eaux Bleues Lake, including sailing, rowing, canoeing, and windsurfing.

33. Explore the Diverse Collection at Blitz

Discover an eclectic array at Blitz, curated by part-time DJ and connoisseur David Bolito. Spread across two floors, this bazaar-gallery offers a fascinating blend of vintage finds, kitsch items, and unique gems. From Toiletpaper calendars to ceramics by artist Séverin Millet, Dolly Parton candles, brutalist mugs, and artisanal cosmetics, Blitz caters to diverse tastes. The top floor features a gallery space hosting rotating pop-up exhibitions, ensuring a fresh experience with each visit.

34. Take in the View from the Jardin Des Curiosités

Experience arguably the most breathtaking view of Lyon from the Jardin Des Curiosités. Perched on a hill in Saint-Just, this 6,000-square-meter park offers a panoramic view worth the uphill climb. Originating from a design commissioned by the city of Montreal, the garden presents a captivating panorama, with the potential to spot Mont Blanc on clear days. Discover hidden treasures, including six chairs designed by Quebecois sculptor Michel Goulet, providing unique lookout points in this enchanting park.

LYON CUSTOMS AND ETIQUETTE

In Lyon, food plays a central role in local culture, with the city boasting a renowned gastronomy. Despite its global culinary reputation, many Lyon residents prefer home-cooked meals over dining out, upholding a strong tradition. Lyon's cultural prominence, now rivaling that of Paris, is evident in Vieux Lyon, a UNESCO World Heritage site and Europe's second-largest Renaissance site. The city hosts over 21,000 events annually, attracting three million tourists during its Festival of Lights.

Georgia Tucker

Language is an integral part of Lyon's identity, with locals primarily speaking French. However, in tourist-centric establishments, English is commonly spoken. Travelers are encouraged to familiarize themselves with basic French phrases, including "bonjour" (hello), "au revoir" (goodbye), "s'il vous plaît" (please), and "merci" (thank you).

The official currency is the euro, with an approximate exchange rate of $1.20 per euro. Travelers can exchange currency at the airport or various locations in Lyon, though it's advisable to check the current rate. Tipping practices include rounding out restaurant bills with a small tip, as service charges are typically included. Additionally, offering a few euros to hotel staff for their services is customary.

Navigating local customs and etiquette is essential for a positive experience in Lyon. Some tips include:

1. **Greetings:** The customary greeting in Lyon involves two kisses on the cheeks, starting with the left. This is observed not only among friends but also in professional interactions.

2. **Dining:** When dining out, it's polite to wait until everyone at the table is served before starting to eat. Keeping hands visible on the table during the meal and expressing gratitude to servers with "please" and "thank you" are considered essential.

What Tradition Did I Learn About?: Understanding the traditional meal structure reveals that Lyon residents rarely eat at restaurants, preferring home-cooked meals. Family meals typically consist of four or more courses, beginning with an aperitif in the family room, followed by a transition to the dining room for the main course served family-style. A baguette is a constant presence, and each meal concludes with a cheese course and dessert.

Why Does the Community Have This Tradition? : The community upholds the tradition of elaborate family meals due to the profound importance placed on family bonds. These extended dining experiences create opportunities for meaningful connections and in-depth conversations among family members. Additionally, the residents of Lyon take immense pride in their culinary skills. Consequently, these lavish meals serve as a platform for them to showcase their exceptional cooking abilities.

Guidelines for Lyon Etiquette:

1. **Dress Code:** Given Lyon's stylish ambiance, it is advisable to dress appropriately. Avoid overly casual or athletic attire and opt for more fashionable clothing to align with the city's standards.

2. **Language:** French is the official language in Lyon. While many locals understand English, making an effort to speak French is highly appreciated by the community.

3. **Tipping Etiquette:** Tipping is not as prevalent in Lyon as in some other regions. However, it is considered courteous to leave a small tip, typically a few euros, for exceptional service.

By adhering to these cultural norms and etiquette guidelines, visitors can ensure a more enjoyable and culturally respectful experience in Lyon.

LYON ON A BUDGET

TRAVEL HACKS TO SAVE ON YOUR TRIP

If a visit to Lyon is on your travel agenda, or you find yourself in the region unsure about budget constraints, fret not. Exploring Lyon on a modest budget is entirely feasible. Numerous strategies can help you make the most of your Lyon experience without straining your

Georgia Tucker

finances. Do not let concerns about your savings hinder an amazing vacation.

A key approach to alleviate travel-related stress is by securely storing your luggage. Our extensive network of luggage storage facilities in Lyon is poised to assist you in this regard. This ensures a hassle-free Lyon trip, unburdened by the weight of cumbersome bags. Many noteworthy destinations like the Lyon Cathedral are less than ideal for managing bulky luggage, and entrusting your belongings to us guarantees a carefree and enjoyable journey.

Cheap Places to Stay In Lyon

Your choice of accommodation significantly influences your travel budget in Lyon. Consulting our guide to the finest neighborhoods in Lyon is advisable before finalizing your hotel selection. For those eager to explore Lyon, accessing and departing from the city center is seamless with these delightful and affordable hotel options.

1. Hôtel du Helder: Situated just across the river from Vieux Lyon, this budget-friendly hotel offers rooms at a modest $50 per night. Remarkably, it is not a hostel, providing guests with private rooms a stone's throw away from the city center. Conveniently located near various public transport options, it is within walking distance of the Rhône River and Place Bellecour Square. The hotel boasts free Wi-Fi, an on-site restaurant (at an additional cost), and air-conditioned rooms—an especially welcome feature during the summer months.

2. ho36 Hostel Lyon: This charming hostel provides access to a bar, lounge, and restaurant, with room rates starting at just $63 per night. Once again, its proximity to Vieux Lyon and key attractions like the Lyon Cathedral and UNESCO World Heritage sites enhances its appeal. Free Wi-Fi, comfortable beds, and affordable dining options contribute to the hostel's welcoming atmosphere.

3. Lagrange Apart'Hôtel - Lyon Lumière: This hotel, designed in an apartment-style format, offers rooms at a reasonable rate of $70 per night. Guests can enjoy the comfort of their apartment-style room, and some spaces are equipped with kitchens and dining areas. Additionally, the hotel features a delightful rooftop terrace with a hot tub. Free Wi-Fi, air-conditioned rooms, and proximity to public transport make it a convenient choice. Its location also allows walking access to key city center attractions, such as the Basilique Notre Dame de Fourvière.

Cheap Things to Do In Lyon

1. Explore the Zoo at Parc de la Tete d'Or: Within the vicinity of the city center, there are numerous affordable and enjoyable activities. A visit to Parc de la Tete d'Or provides opportunities to experience lush green spaces, relax in shaded areas, and savor snacks obtained from local street food vendors. The park is also home to a sizable zoo, which offers free admission—a perfect option for those traveling with children.

2. Notre Dame de Fourvière: The Notre Dame de Fourvière church is open to visitors without an entrance fee, with the option to enhance the experience through an audio tour priced at $16. The audio tour provides valuable insights into the religious history of the city and the Vieux Lyon district. Perched atop Fourvière Hill, the church offers breathtaking views of its UNESCO World Heritage surroundings. Exploring Notre Dame de Fourvière is a uniquely enriching experience that should not be overlooked.

Georgia Tucker

3. Discover Vieux Lyon: Venture to Vieux Lyon to access the city's oldest section, featuring the medieval Cathédrale Saint-Jean-Baptiste, various museums, and other tourist attractions. The area is conveniently connected to Fourvière Hill and St-Just through funiculars, allowing visitors to explore multiple attractions in a single day for a nominal fee of approximately €2. The funicular ride offers spectacular views, enhancing the overall experience.

Cheap Places to Eat in Lyon

If you enjoy dining outdoors, Lyon's street food scene offers an excellent and cost-effective choice. It's worth noting that opting for takeout and enjoying meals in your hotel room on certain nights can be a smart way to save money during your stay. If your accommodation includes kitchen facilities or communal cooking spaces, cooking your own meals is also a viable option. Here are some recommended budget-friendly restaurants:

1. La Cocagne: This charming French gastronomy venue is surprisingly affordable. Experience delightful local wines, delicious French cuisine, and fusion favorites with Asian-inspired flair. La Cocagne is an ideal choice for an elegant dinner without straining your budget. Anticipate spending around €20 per person or €30 with beverages. The service is efficient and friendly, and the expertly prepared traditional dishes cater to a variety of tastes.

2. Food Tours: While not a specific dining location, a food tour provides the opportunity to sample offerings from various local eateries and indulge in delightful regional wines. These tours are reasonably priced, with costs varying. On most tours, you can dine at different establishments across the city for approximately €40 per person. The tour company handles transportation, and some drinks and tastings are complimentary at the visited locations. Embark on a journey to Lyon with the goal to explore French gastronomy and savor local wines.

3. La Tête de Lard: For homemade dishes at an excellent value, La Tête de Lard is the go-to place for a satisfying meal. The welcoming atmosphere treats patrons like family, and the Lyonnaise specialties on the menu are unique to this establishment. Generous portions ensure you can dine here for under €20 without compromising on quality. Traditional yet cost-effective, these restaurants are a perfect choice for those looking to save money while relishing each meal.

Cheap Bars in Lyon

If you're looking to save money on a night out, especially if you have other costly experiences planned, these bars offer a budget-friendly option without compromising on the enjoyable moments you anticipated during your trip to France.

1. L'Abreuvoir: This charming tavern provides reasonably priced beer and delightful snacks like sausage. A pint here typically costs around €3, and the food is also affordable. While the venue is small, it offers a cozy setting for you to enjoy with friends and family. L'Abreuvoir is the type of place that comes to mind when thinking about a night out in Lyon, ensuring a great time.

2. Groom: Hostel bars are excellent spots to save money while having a night out. If the prices in the old town seem a bit steep, head to Groom for cocktails, beer, and a lively atmosphere. This venue attracts a younger crowd, making it a haven for budget-conscious

Georgia Tucker

travelers. You're sure to have a fantastic time with this energetic and laid-back crowd.

3. L'Antisèche: Doubling as an eatery, this small bar is a viable option for both dinner and drinks. Cocktails and beer here are priced at less than €5, and a comprehensive food menu is available. The atmosphere is casual, allowing you to take your time without feeling rushed, unlike some other smaller venues.

Bonus Budget Tips for Lyon

1. Lyon City Card: Ensure you acquire the Lyon City Card before embarking on your city center and downtown adventures. It's advisable to order in advance online, securing a 10% discount. This invaluable card grants free entry to 23 museums across the city, includes a complimentary guided walking tour and provides access to a free river cruise—an unbeatable value. Incorporating the Lyon City Card into your travel plans streamlines your Lyon experience, making it an essential aspect of trip organization.

2. Delve into History: For enthusiasts of Roman history, Lyon offers various sites within the ancient city where you can immerse yourself in the history of Lugdunum. These UNESCO World Heritage sites are affordably accessible, allowing history buffs to uncover fascinating stories scattered throughout the charming old town.

3. Walking: Tours Guided tours need not break the bank in Lyon. Exploring your options may reveal local guides offering free walking tours, typically concluding with a voluntary tip. Locals, well-versed in the largest city in this region of France, often provide more insightful tours than some recommended tour companies, offering a cost-effective way to discover the city's attractions.

4. Travel During the Off-Season: Consider planning your Lyon visit during the off-season, particularly between February and May, when hotel prices are more budget-friendly. Since accommodation expenses can significantly impact your overall budget, choosing a month with lower costs allows you to allocate more funds to explore the diverse attractions scattered throughout the city.

5. Explore La Croix-Rousse: The bohemian La Croix-Rousse neighborhood beckons for a leisurely afternoon of exploration. Tree-lined streets create a picturesque setting, ideal for strolling on warm days. Steeped in history, every corner of this older district tells a story. Don't be surprised to encounter street performers and other captivating activities as you meander through this charming part of the city.

THINGS TO DO IN LYON FOR FREE OR ON A SMALL BUDGET

Even with a modest budget, Lyon offers an enriching vacation experience. The UNESCO World Heritage-listed historic center presents a charming neighborhood filled with hidden passages, affordable dining options, and magnificent historical landmarks and churches.

In addition to the Old Town, Lyon provides various cost-free activities: wander through Parc de la Tête d'Or, unwind along the Rhône River in the evening, delve into the city's Roman history, and more. Discover below why Lyon vacations need not be financially burdensome.

1. Get a Lyon City Card

For those intending to thoroughly explore Lyon and its attractions, the City Card proves to be a cost-effective choice. Available for durations ranging from 1 to 4 days, it grants access to all city public transport modes—bus, tram, metro, Velo'v, and funicular. Moreover, it offers complimentary admission or discounted entry to over 50 attractions. It's crucial to note that if you don't plan to visit many attractions, the Lyon City Card might not be necessary. In such cases, the 1-day City Pass ('Ticket Liberté 1 Jour' in French) provides better value for those seeking discounts on transportation alone.

2. Lyon Cathedral and Other Churches

Lyon's city center boasts an array of exquisite religious structures. Alongside the Basilica of Notre-Dame de Fourvière and the Cathedral of Saint John the Baptist, the Old Town hosts four churches. Noteworthy among them are Saint-Nizier Church on Rue Saint-Nizier, Saint-George Church on Quai Fulchiron, and Saint-Martin d'Ainay Abbey on Rue Bourgelat. Regardless of your religious inclinations, the architecture and embellishments of these places are sure to captivate.

3. Explore the Parc de la Tête d'Or

Situated north of the city center along the River Saône, Parc de la Tête d'Or stands as one of France's largest urban public parks. Besides its extensive network of paths for jogging and cycling, the park encompasses a botanical garden and a zoo, both accessible at no cost. Additionally, affordable activities such as boating on the lake, riding the mini train, and enjoying the carousel are available. The park also hosts restaurants and snack stalls.

4. Walk up Fourvière Hill

Embark on a hike to the summit of Fourvière Hill to relish panoramic views of Lyon. Once atop, explore the impressive 19th-century Basilica of Notre-Dame de Fourvière, a prominent city landmark. If the hike seems challenging, an alternative is the funicular ride to the top, with a single ticket priced at less than EUR 2. Worth noting: the funicular journey is inclusive of the cost of a public transport 1-Day City Pass ('Ticket Liberté 1 Jour' in French).

Location: Place de Fourvière, 69005 Lyon, France

5. Lose Yourself in Lyon's Old Town Traboules

Discover Lyon's Old Town and the Croix-Rousse district through the enchanting traboules—a network of hidden passageways. These covered corridors weave through the historic buildings, connecting streets discreetly. An iconic feature of Lyon, approximately 40 traboules are open to the public. Obtain a map of these passages at the Office of Tourism on Bellecourt Square for a self-guided exploration, or opt for guided tours available for a more in-depth experience.

Location: Lyon's Old Town and Croix-Rousse district

6. Wander in the Confluence District

Located at the convergence of the Saône and Rhône Rivers, the Confluence district, positioned at the southern tip of the Presqu'île, has undergone a remarkable transformation from an industrial zone to a modern hub. This area, now adorned with innovative architecture, features a significant shopping mall, restaurants, nightlife, and boutiques. A highlight is the Museum of the Confluences, a science center and anthropology museum with an entrance fee of EUR 9 per adult.

Location: La Confluence, 69002 Lyon, France

7. Go Shopping at Les Puces du Canal

Experience the charm of Les Puces du Canal (the Canal Flea Market), held thrice weekly in Villeurbanne, 5 km northeast of the city center. Boasting approximately 400 stalls, this vast market offers an eclectic array of goods, from clothing to furniture and household items. Sharpen your bargaining skills for great deals amidst a convivial atmosphere, with on-site restaurants, cafes, and a bakery.

Location: 3 Rue Eugène Pottier, 69100 Villeurbanne, France

Open: Thursdays (7 am to 1 pm), Saturdays (9 am to 1 pm), Sundays (7 am to 3 pm)

8. Must-See: The Gallo-Roman Theatre and Odeon

Witness the timeless allure of the Gallo-Roman Theatre and Odeon, constructed between 15 BC and the 1st century AD and still in use for cultural events. These UNESCO World Heritage sites, remnants of the ancient city of Lugdunum, host up to 13,000 people with free entry. Adjacent is a museum dedicated to the Roman occupation of Lyon, accessible free of charge on Thursdays.

Location: 17 Rue Cléberg, 69005 Lyon, France

Open: April 15 – September 15 (7 am to 9 pm), September 16 – April 14 (7 am to 7 pm)

9. Eat well for less in Lyon Downtown

Lyon, renowned as the French epicenter of exceptional cuisine, beckons with its array of delectable yet budget-friendly dining options. Here are three recommended restaurants in the city center for your culinary delight. Indulge in the diverse sandwich offerings crafted with local ingredients at Gourmix Terreaux on Rue de la Platière. For a tantalizing array of tartines—generous slices of bread with various toppings—visit Restaurant L'Epicerie on Rue de la Monnaie. Across the Rhone River, savor authentic local cuisine in a convivial ambiance at Le Bistrot des Fauves on Rue Saint-Michel.

10. Enjoy a bottle of Beaujolais on the banks of the Rhône River

A delightful 5 km promenade along the Rhône River's east bank provides a charming evening retreat. Elevate your experience by acquiring a bottle of local wine, such as Beaujolais or Côte-du-Rhône, and find a comfortable spot along the embankment. Immerse yourself in the tranquil ambiance, sip your chosen wine, and relish the view of the Old Town against the backdrop of the illuminated city lights, creating a particularly enchanting scene at night.

Georgia Tucker

CHAPTER NINE: SAFETY

A COMPREHENSIVE SAFETY GUIDE

As the third-largest city in France, Lyon boasts a rich history rooted in Roman origins, offering captivating experiences ranging from Roman amphitheaters to medieval and Renaissance architecture. Recognized as a UNESCO World Heritage Site, Lyon is a cultural hub connecting northern and southern Europe. Birthplace of cinema, the city hosts unique film and music festivals, along with exceptional shopping and antique markets.

With an abundance of attractions, the question arises: Is Lyon safe to visit? The overarching answer is affirmative, and this comprehensive safety guide will provide insights for worry-free exploration. To fully enjoy the sights without concern, entrust your belongings to a secure Bounce storage site in Lyon, allowing you to immerse yourself in the cultural richness and experiences the city has to offer.

Is Lyon Safe to Visit Right Now?

With a 2023 Global Peace Index rating of 55 for France, Lyon stands as a secure destination, even for solo travelers. Given its popularity among tourists, taking proactive measures can enhance your safety and protect your belongings.

Common challenges faced by tourists include pickpocketing and scams, but armed with knowledge about Lyon's safety measures, you can fully enjoy your stay in this enchanting region of France. Understanding how to blend in and avoid drawing attention to yourself is a key aspect of personal safety.

While no safety guide is infallible, conducting thorough research and consulting your government's official travel guidelines for both France and Lyon before finalizing your plans is strongly advised.

Safety in Lyon's Public Transportation

Lyon's public transport system is generally considered safe for tourists. As a bustling city, Lyon features the TGV Duplex, a two-level high-speed train connecting Lyon and Paris. While the experience might be intense, especially on the upper level, it offers a swift journey to your destination.

Lyon, known for its walkable streets, encourages visitors to opt for public transportation over driving to navigate the crowded thoroughfares. The city's public transport system is both functional and reliable.

For those choosing the metro over walking, it is crucial to purchase tickets from authorized agents or the metro station's kiosk. Beware of counterfeit metro tickets, a common scam. Automated service stations ensure a secure transaction, minimizing the risk of falling victim to scams.

Emergency Numbers in Lyon

While the likelihood of encountering issues on Lyon is low, being aware of essential emergency phone numbers is prudent. Store them in your phone or alongside important documents. Additionally, note your country's embassy contact details and keep them with your passport.

- European emergency number: 112

- Health emergency: 15

- Police (available 24/7): 17

Ensuring Personal Safety in Lyon

As Lyon hosts renowned international events like film and music festivals, attracting massive crowds annually, it remains one of France's beloved cities. Recognized for its charm, Lyon is a must-visit destination. The city's public transport system, although straightforward, merits a quick review in "How to Get Around Lyon" before your arrival.

For female solo travelers, Lyon promises a safe and thrilling experience, offering captivating Roman and Medieval sites alongside modern architectural marvels in the city's newer sections.

Solo Travel in Lyon: Safety Guidelines

According to the Bounce Women Travel Safety Index, France receives a safety rating of 14. While caution is advisable for solo travelers, Lyon is generally considered safe for those exploring on their own. Female solo travelers, in particular, can feel at ease when visiting various cities in France.

To enhance safety, adopt a few key practices: travel light, choose accommodations in tourist-friendly neighborhoods, and dress inconspicuously to avoid standing out as a tourist. Develop a detailed itinerary and share it with a friend or family member. Seek recommendations from hostel or hotel staff regarding places to visit, and keep them informed about your whereabouts. Keep your mobile phone readily accessible and familiarize yourself with Lyon's emergency numbers, including 112, equivalent to 911 in the USA.

Georgia Tucker

COMMON CRIMES AND SCAMS TO BEWARE OF IN LYON

While Lyon is relatively safe, there are common crimes and scams to be aware of, particularly around tourist attractions. Stay vigilant in public spaces, especially if you are easily identifiable as a tourist.

Pickpocketing: Vieux Lyon, in particular, attracts professional thieves targeting tourists, especially those with cameras or large bags. Stay alert, carry only essential items, and dress inconspicuously to blend in. Utilizing a Bounce storage facility can be a practical solution, allowing you to carry fewer items and enjoy peace of mind.

Scam Risks: Common scams involve fake charity petitions, where individuals distribute misleading pamphlets to solicit immediate donations. Refrain from giving cash to street fundraisers, even if their cause seems genuine. The gold ring trick is another scam to be wary of; individuals may offer you a supposedly found gold ring and then demand payment. Politely decline any objects offered by strangers on the street to avoid potential scams.

SAFEST NEIGHBORHOODS IN LYON

In Lyon, the neighborhoods are generally known for their safety, with Vieux Lyon standing out as a charming area and La Presqu'Ile as the central hub.

Vieux Lyon: Vieux Lyon boasts an iconic, medieval ambiance, offering captivating attractions. Positioned as the true heart of the city, it provides stunning vistas of the hills and Alps near the Swiss border. The neighborhood features a blend of entertainment and shopping opportunities, making it a vibrant choice.

La Presqu'Ile: Situated in the UNESCO World Heritage district, La Presqu'Ile is one of Lyon's premier neighborhoods. Its name, translating to "peninsula" in English, signifies its location at the confluence of the Rhone and Saone Rivers. Recognized as the city center, La Presqu'Ile houses splendid shops and restaurants. Notably, Rue de la Republique, a vital commercial street, resides here, ensuring excellent metro connections and proximity to key attractions. The area remains lively day and night, adding an enjoyable dimension to your stay.

3e Arrondissement: Adjacent to the city center on the east bank of the Rhone River, the Third District is akin to Downtown Lyon. It stands out as one of Lyon's most populous and diverse neighborhoods, featuring modern landmarks like Tour Incity, Tour Swiss Life, Tour Part-Dieu, and Tour Oxygène. Particularly suitable for business travelers, the Third District offers extensive public transportation options, including Metro lines B and D, facilitating easy exploration across Lyon. Affordable lodging choices further enhance the appeal of this neighborhood.

Georgia Tucker

CHAPTER TEN: ITINERARY OPTIONS

2 DAYS ITINERARY

Lyon, a city gaining popularity among travelers, particularly stands out as France's gastronomic capital. Offering a delightful blend of excellent cuisine, history, culture, and tradition, Lyon captivates visitors globally. In this 2-day itinerary, we'll guide you through activities, places to explore, and culinary delights, ensuring you make the most of your brief 48 hours in this enchanting destination.

City Highlights: With a history spanning over 2,000 years, Lyon's UNESCO World Heritage site, Vieux Lyon (Old Town), awaits your exploration. Immerse yourself in the well-preserved Renaissance architecture and charming cobblestone streets during your visit.

Day 1 In Lyon

Georgia Tucker

Explore The Historic Vieux Lyon

Begin your journey by exploring Vieux Lyon, the city's oldest district and a protected site under the Marlaux law. While the Presquile became Lyon's modern center, Vieux Lyon retains its historical charm with intact buildings and courtyards. Traverse narrow cobblestone alleys to glimpse into the city's past. Discover hidden passageways known as traboules, once used by silk merchants, adding a touch of mystery to the area.

Check Out the Basilica of Notre-Dame De Fourviere

Embark on a morning tour to the majestic Basilica of Notre-Dame de Fourvière, perched atop Fourvière Hill. Designed by renowned architects Pierre Bossan and Sainte-Marie Perrin, this UNESCO World Heritage site serves as the city's emblem. Dedicated to the Virgin Mary, the basilica welcomes over 2.5 million pilgrims annually. Beyond its spiritual significance, Notre Dame offers breathtaking panoramic views of the city. Explore its grand interiors, adorned with intricate mosaics, ornate stained-glass windows, and historical significance, making it a must-visit during your stay.

Get Lunch at Paul Bocuse

As previously noted, Lyon holds the esteemed title of France's gastronomic capital, boasting numerous Michelin-starred restaurants, including the renowned Paul Bocuse. A visit to Lyon would be incomplete without savoring the gastronomic offerings at this establishment, named after the legendary French chef. Located just minutes from Notre-Dame, Paul Bocuse provides an opportunity to sample exquisite dishes crafted with the finest local and seasonal ingredients, employing innovative culinary techniques.

See Place Bellecour

Situated as one of Europe's largest squares, Place Bellecour stands as a prominent landmark in Lyon. This central hub of the historic city center, once a Roman military square, is now recognized as a UNESCO World Heritage Site and a popular tourist destination with rich historical implications. A leisurely stroll through the area unveils iconic statuaries, sculptures, and notable landmarks, such as the central equestrian statue of Louis XIV, the Saone and Rhone figures, the Stone Watchmen, and the renowned Antoine de Saint Exupery statue. Surrounding the square, you'll find beautiful buildings, luxury boutiques, and cafes, making it a delightful place to explore. Throughout the year, the square hosts significant events, from book fairs and public concerts to local festivals.

Admire The Cathédrale Saint-Jean-Baptiste

Following your exploration of Lyon's bustling square, your next destination is the imposing Cathédrale Saint-Jean-Baptiste. Serving as both a place of worship and a testament to Lyon's rich history and architectural heritage, this cathedral remains the seat of the city's archbishop. Positioned in a waterfront plaza near the Saone of Old Lyon, the cathedral, known as the Primate of the Gauls, captivates visitors with its magnificent architectural blend of Gothic and Romanesque styles. The interior and exterior, crafted over centuries, showcase remarkable craftsmanship. Noteworthy is the cathedral's famous astronomical clock, which offers an hourly show for visitors' delight. Take your time to explore the serene courtyard and the adjacent archaeological garden, adding to the cathedral's allure.

Discover Lyon's Famous Traboules

While you may chance upon a few traboules during your visit to Vieux Lyon, allocating time (approximately one to two hours)

Georgia Tucker

specifically for exploring these passages is essential during your two days in Lyon. These concealed walkways are a distinctive feature of Lyon, offering insights into the city's rich history and culture. Initially employed by silk merchants for transporting goods, the traboules are now open for exploration.

As you delve into these pathways, unveil hidden courtyards, intricate staircases, and exquisite Renaissance-era facades. Certain traboules lead to concealed treasures such as small gardens or charming shops, enhancing the overall sense of discovery. Traboules can be found across Vieux Lyon, Croix-Rousse, and various other parts of the city. However, it's worth noting that only about 5% of these passages are accessible and navigable, as some property owners have closed off certain traboules.

Visit The Museum of Fine Arts of Lyon
While the focus of day one revolves around exploring the historical aspects of the city, it's imperative to visit the Museum of Fine Arts before the day concludes. Lyon takes pride in its rich historical heritage and is home to numerous museums showcasing diverse arts and culture. Art enthusiasts, as well as those less familiar with the art world, should seize the opportunity to explore the Museum of Fine Arts of Lyon.

Housed in a grand 17th-century edifice, the museum boasts an extensive collection of artworks spanning various periods and styles. Among the masterpieces on display are works by renowned artists such as Monet, Renoir, Picasso, and Van Gogh. The museum also features sculptures, decorative arts, and archaeological artifacts.

Dine & Drink at the Groom

Following your exploration of Lyon's attractions, indulge in a memorable dining and drinking experience at one of its premier establishments, Groom. This chic and lively venue seamlessly combines gastronomy with mixology, offering a unique fusion. While Lyon boasts several bars and restaurants, Groom stands out as a favorite among both travelers and locals.

This trendy and upscale bar presents modern cocktails, a lineup of live music, and local DJs every night. The carefully crafted menu blends traditional French flavors with contemporary twists. Whether you're seeking a vibrant night out in Lyon or aiming to savor a delightful dinner, Groom stands as the ideal destination.

Day 2 in Lyon

Leisurely Walk at Parc De La Tête d'Or

Embark on your second day in Lyon with a stroll at the city's most significant urban park, Parc de la Tête d'Or. While the park is accessible throughout the day, we recommend a morning visit to immerse yourself in the serenity and tranquility it offers. This expansive urban oasis boasts lush green spaces, serene lakes, and picturesque walking paths. Additionally, the park features various attractions, including a zoo, a lake, and even a miniature railroad.

For those seeking more active pursuits, the park offers kilometers of trails for hiking, as well as open fields for running and playing. Alternatively, take a more relaxed approach, pause at a nearby café for coffee and pastries, and relish in a brief picnic.

Georgia Tucker

Explore Place des Jacobins

Experience one of France's most iconic and beautiful squares in Lyon – the Place des Jacobins. Originally part of the Jacobin convent, the square underwent transformation after its initial destruction, now adorned with a striking white marble fountain. The fountain serves as the centerpiece, representing four renowned French artists.

As you stroll through the square, understanding its historical narrative adds depth to your appreciation of the harmonious blend of historical and contemporary elements. Take a moment to admire the bronze statue of King Louis XIV at the fountain's center and marvel at the facades embellished with ornate balconies and balconettes.

Have Brunch at Halles De Lyon

Indulge in another delightful brunch experience at Halles de Lyon, a renowned food market showcasing the best of Lyon's gastronomy. A must-visit in Lyon, the market's stalls abound with fresh produce, artisanal cheeses, cured meats, and tempting pastries. Explore the area, curate a selection of delectable treats, and find a cozy spot to savor your brunch.

Sample local specialties such as quenelles, saucissons, and creamy cheeses, or seek recommendations from locals for new culinary experiences. Engaging in conversations with friendly vendors reveals their passion for the culinary arts, offering insights into why Lyon is hailed as the gastronomy capital of France.

Visit Amphithéâtre des Trois Gaules

Amphithéâtre des Trois Gaules stands as another pivotal landmark in Lyon, holding significant historical importance. Formerly known as Lugdunum, it served as a gathering and entertainment venue during the Roman era. The theatre gained prominence as the Gauls congregated here for assemblies, influencing politics, religion, and social dynamics.

The well-preserved ruins now provide an exploration site for both locals and visitors. Admire the remaining stone seating tiers and the partially reconstructed stage, gaining insights into Roman architectural prowess. Additionally, an on-site museum offers a deeper understanding of its history. While guided tours are available, independent exploration is equally viable.

Spend Time at The Museum of Cinema and Miniatures

Discover one of Lyon's premier interactive museums, the Museum of Cinema and Miniatures, renowned not only in Lyon but throughout France. After immersing yourself in history and culture, unleash your inner film enthusiast within the museum's captivating collection of cinema artifacts.

Inside, you'll encounter a fascinating array of props, costumes, and set designs from iconic movies. Marvel at the meticulous details and craftsmanship of miniature models that intricately bring famous film scenes to life, evoking awe and wonder. The museum boasts different galleries, each adorned with memorabilia from both classic and contemporary films. Advance bookings open the door to workshops and demonstrations, providing insights into the techniques and processes involved.

Take A Cruise at Saône River

Before concluding your 48-hour Lyon journey, seize the opportunity to experience one of the city's highlights – a scenic cruise on the Saône River. With the city embracing this beautiful waterway, board a riverboat for a leisurely cruise, offering a fresh perspective on Lyon's landmarks and picturesque landscapes.

Numerous charters await to navigate the Saône River, providing a relaxing journey as you absorb panoramic views. Opting for a sunset cruise enhances the experience, allowing you to witness the sky's changing hues and culminating in a captivating view of the illuminated city at night.

Dinner At Takao Takano

Wrap up your adventurous day with a gourmet dining experience at Takao Takano, a Michelin-starred restaurant. Offering a fusion of traditional French cuisine and innovative Japanese flavors, Chef Takao Takano crafts exquisite dishes that embody his unique culinary vision.

Anticipate each plate to be a masterpiece, seamlessly blending flavors, textures, and techniques for an unforgettable gastronomic journey. The restaurant's elegant ambiance and impeccable service enhance your dining experience, ensuring a memorable evening as you conclude your trip.

Tours In Lyon

Food Tour

Delve deeper into the city's culinary culture by participating in a Food Tour in Lyon. Guided by a local expert, explore the Old Town's hidden gems where you can savor authentic local cuisine. The tour takes you to five restaurants, bakeries, and artisan shops in a small group setting, offering a taste of Lyonnaise specialties like Pike quenelle, Cervelle des Canuts, and Pink Praline Brioche.

As you indulge in these delightful treats, benefit from valuable tips and insights shared by your knowledgeable local guide, enhancing your understanding of Lyon's rich culinary heritage.

Guided Walking Tour

Explore Lyon through the Highlights & Secrets Walking Guided Tour, a captivating option that showcases the city's significant landmarks, including Place des Terreaux, Vieux Lyon, and Colline de Fourviere. This tour unveils major tourist destinations, providing insights shared by a knowledgeable local guide. What sets it apart is the discovery of secret routes, a unique aspect revealed exclusively to participants.

2-Day Itinerary for Lyon Wrap-Up

That concludes our comprehensive 2-day Lyon itinerary! Armed with the knowledge of what you can accomplish in just 48 hours in the city, any doubts about this trip can be put to rest. With meticulous planning and scheduling, you are poised for an enriching adventure in Lyon.

A COMPLETE 1 DAY ITINERARY

Lyon, the third-largest city in France and the capital of Auvergne-Rhône-Alpes, boasts a rich history spanning 2,000 years. From the Roman Amphithéâtre des Trois Gaules and medieval charm in Vieux Lyon to the modern Confluence district, Lyon's center is a tapestry of historical and architectural wonders. What began as a visit to a friend turned into an unexpectedly enjoyable experience.

Georgia Tucker

Explore Lyon in a Day

Stop 1: Ancient Theatre of Fourvière (Teatro Galo-Romano)
Discover the Roman Amphithéâtre des Trois Gaules, a UNESCO World Heritage Site, located on the hill of Fourvière in the heart of the Roman City. Open daily from 07:00 to 19:00, with the museum accessible Tuesday to Friday (11:00-18:00), weekends (10:00-18:00), and the library open Tuesday to Friday (13:00-17:00). Museum admission is €4, with free entry on the first Sunday of each month. Tickets can be purchased on-site or online, taking approximately 30 minutes for this visit.

Stop 2: The Basilica of Notre-Dame de Fourvière
Visit La Basilique Notre Dame de Fourvière, a splendid minor basilica constructed in Lyon from 1872 to 1896. Positioned strategically with a breathtaking view of the city, the basilica welcomes visitors daily from 07:00 to 20:00. Allocate approximately 15 minutes for this stop.

Stop 3: Saint-Jean-Baptiste Cathedral
Explore Lyon Cathedral, a Roman Catholic church on Place Saint-Jean in central Lyon. Dedicated to Saint John the Baptist, this architectural marvel, completed in 1476, serves as the Archbishop of Lyon's seat. Open on weekdays (08:15-19:45), Saturdays (08:15-19:00), and Sundays (08:00-19:45), the cathedral offers a 15-minute exploration.

Stop 4: Museum of Cinema and Miniature
Experience the fascinating Museum of Cinema and Miniature, featuring hyper-realistic miniature scenes and exhibits on movie

props and special effects. Often overlooked, this hidden gem captivates visitors for 1 to 2 hours, making it a must-visit in Lyon.

Stop 5: Old Lyon (Vieux Lyon)
Discover the charm of Vieux Lyon, the city's largest Renaissance district and its oldest. A leisurely walk through its historic streets provides a calming experience, with numerous cafés and restaurants to explore. The duration of your stay in this captivating district is flexible, allowing you to enjoy a meal or drink at your own pace.

Stop 6: Bellecour Square (Place Bellecour)
Immerse yourself in the grandeur of Place Bellecour, one of Europe's largest open squares and the third-largest in France. Take your time to explore, and feel free to relax at nearby cafés or restaurants. The duration of your visit here is flexible, offering the perfect opportunity to savor a meal or refreshment.

LYON'S TRAVEL APPS FOR YOUR CONVENIENCE
Enhance your Lyon experience with English language apps designed to assist you in organizing your trip, facilitating journeys, and ensuring a seamless stay. Download your preferred apps now for both iPhone and Android devices.

Discovery Apps
1. **Enform@Lyon:** Explore Lyon's heritage sites at your own pace with the Enform@Lyon app. Created by the City of Lyon, it offers audioguided running or walking routes, categorized by difficulty (green, blue, or red). New tours are regularly added, featuring video-based muscle strengthening sessions with three difficulty levels. You can customize your experience by activating or

deactivating comments and videos. All trails are accessible to individuals with reduced mobility, making it an ideal way to stay active while discovering Lyon.

2. **Cityscape:** Gain a comprehensive understanding of the city, its developments, and urban landscaping with the Cityscape app. Whether you want information about a building or guidance on a specific route, this app provides the necessary tools. It serves as a valuable resource for those interested in exploring the city's architectural and urban features.

3. **Teazit:** Rediscover Lyon through Teazit, a community-driven app featuring video teasers of various venues, including bars, art galleries, clubs, and restaurants. The app offers a glimpse into the atmosphere of each location and showcases ongoing events. Teazit's user-friendly video tool allows you to create and share your teaser with the community, providing a simple and free way to engage with the vibrant life of Lyon.

4. **JOOKS:** Immerse yourself in Lyon by running or walking along pre-established routes tailored to different parts of the city. JOOKS offers routes suitable for various fitness levels, paces, and preferences. Additionally, the app provides cycling routes and a wheelchair-friendly route created in collaboration with Handicap International.

Culture Apps

1. **Fête des Lumières (Festival of Lights):** Stay informed about all installations and tours during the Festival of Lights with this app. Easily share your selected highlights with friends to enhance your collective experience of this dazzling event.

2. **Musée des Beaux-Art:** Experience the Musée des Beaux-Art in total freedom with this app, available in French and English.

Explore over 300 works of art through audio presentations, visuals, texts, and videos. The app includes an interactive map and thematic routes, offering three trails enriched with videos: Works of Art, Colour/Black, and Nature/Plants.

Shopping Apps

1. **Westfield La Part-Dieu Shopping Centre:** Access maps, itineraries, cinema schedules, film trailers, shop news, promotions, and events at Westfield La Part-Dieu shopping centre through this app. Stay updated and make the most of your shopping experience.

2. **Confluence Shopping and Leisure Centre:** Keep track of opening hours, shop information, promotions, cinema schedules, and the shopping centre's layout on your smartphone with this app dedicated to Confluence shopping and leisure centre. Stay well-informed for a seamless shopping experience.

Practical Apps

1. **Ville de Lyon:** Access the official application of the city of Lyon to check swimming pool schedules, stay updated on the latest news, or discover ideas for a leisurely walk.

2. **Toilet Finder:** Ensure a seamless city exploration by knowing the locations of public toilets. Download the Toilet Finder app from Google Play or the App Store for convenient access.

Transport Apps

1. **TCL:** Plan and memorize your TCL bus, metro, tramway, or funicular itineraries with the TCL app. Stay informed about real-

Georgia Tucker

time timetables, route options, potential disruptions, and even purchase tickets online if you have an NFC-equipped Android smartphone.

2. **Taxi Lyon:** Easily book a taxi in and around Lyon using the Taxi Lyon app for hassle-free transportation.

3. **Allbikesnow:** For bicycle enthusiasts, Allbikesnow provides useful assistance in locating bikes through bike-share systems or finding available spaces to return bicycles at stations near your location.

4. **LPA – Lyon Parc Auto:** Use the LPA app to locate the nearest Lyon Parc Auto (LPA) car park and check its real-time availability.

5. **Aéroport de Lyon Saint-Exupéry:** Stay updated on departing and arriving flights in real time, access transportation options to Lyon-Saint-Exupéry airport, book parking spaces, and find the right terminal and services using the Aéroport de Lyon Saint-Exupéry app.

6. **Rhônexpress:** View schedules, purchase tickets, receive information on traffic conditions, and stay informed about flight and train times at Lyon-Saint-Exupéry airport with the Rhônexpress app. You can also enjoy reading the latest novels while waiting. Download it on the App Store or Google Play.

ESSENTIAL APPS FOR NEWCOMERS IN LYON

1. Citymapper: Citymapper is a must-have app for newcomers in Lyon. It not only provides directions from point A to point B but also accurately reflects subway intervals, crucial for navigating Lyon's well-connected metro system. Ideal for newcomers starting their Lyon exploration.

2. Lime: During busy hours, particularly around 8 am and 5 pm when the metros are crowded with people commuting to and from offices, consider utilizing the Lime app. This app allows you to access neon green-colored electric scooters scattered throughout the city. Simply scan the QR code on the scooter using the app, don the helmet, and smoothly travel to your destination. Upon arrival, scan the QR code again to securely lock the scooter, ensuring responsible parking for the next user.

3. Deliveroo: Given Lyon's reputation as a gastronomical city, we feature two food-related apps, starting with Deliveroo. After downloading the app, input your zip code, and it will present a comprehensive list of outstanding restaurants available for delivery in your area. Choose your desired food items and place your order. Noteworthy features include real-time order tracking on your mobile device and the convenience of scheduling food deliveries up to 24 hours in advance.

4. La Fourchette: When you're in the mood for a sophisticated Friday night out but encounter fully booked restaurants, turn to La Fourchette. This app simplifies the reservation process, allowing you to secure a spot even without a fixed date. Additionally, La Fourchette offers exclusive promotions, and as a member, you accumulate points with each booking. The more you dine, the more points you earn.

5. Le Monde: For staying informed about all things French, Le Monde is the go-to app. With a 75-year history, this publication extensively covers French politics, economics, and culture. Whether you're planning a move to Lyon or simply want to stay updated on the current state of the country, reading Le Monde provides valuable insights. Additionally, the newspaper version is likely the only French newspaper accessible in non-French-speaking countries.

Georgia Tucker

CONCLUSION

As we arrive at the final pages of the LYON TRAVEL GUIDE 2024, we trust that the anticipation for your Lyon adventure has been kindled and the allure of this culinary capital has taken root in your wanderlust-filled heart. Throughout this guide, you've delved into the gastronomic wonders, explored historical gems, and absorbed the cultural richness that makes Lyon a jewel in the tapestry of France. As you prepare to bid adieu to Lyon, allow us to leave you with some parting reflections and a sense of fulfillment for the extraordinary journey that awaits.

Lyon's culinary symphony, composed of exquisite flavors and culinary traditions, will continue to resonate in your memories long after you've left its charming streets. Whether you indulged in a decadent Lyonnais meal at a traditional Bouchon or savored a croissant from a local patisserie, the tastes of Lyon are etched into your culinary travelogue. As you return home, carry the essence of Lyon's gastronomic prowess with you and let it inspire your future culinary adventures.

Lyon is not just a city; it's a living canvas where history, culture, and architecture converge to create a timeless masterpiece. The glimpses of the UNESCO-listed Old Town, the panoramic views from Fourvière Hill, and the winding traboules will remain vivid in your memory. Lyon's timeless beauty invites you to relive your experiences in daydreams and beckons you to return and discover even more of its enchanting facets.

Our guide has aimed to be more than just a roadmap; it has been your ticket to experiencing Lyon like a local. The hidden gems, insider tips, and cultural insights were curated to enrich your journey beyond the surface. We hope you embraced Lyon's spirit, engaged with its people, and reveled in the joy of discovery that

Georgia Tucker

comes from navigating the city's cobblestone streets with an insider's perspective.

As you reflect on your Lyon adventure, we trust that the LYON TRAVEL GUIDE 2024 played a pivotal role in making your trip seamless and enjoyable. From the initial stages of planning to the moment you step into this vibrant city, our guide aims to provide you with the knowledge and tools to navigate Lyon with confidence and ease. We hope it becomes a companion, a source of inspiration, and a key to unlocking Lyon's many secrets.

On behalf of our dedicated team, we express our deepest gratitude for choosing the LYON TRAVEL GUIDE 2024 as your companion on this extraordinary journey. Lyon is a city of revelations, a place where every corner tells a story and every meal is an experience. We hope our guide has empowered you to create lasting memories, forge connections, and immerse yourself in the magic that is Lyon.

Lyon awaits your return, ready to welcome you with open arms and new adventures. As you close the final chapter of this guide, remember that Lyon's charm is not confined to these pages; it's a living, breathing entity that continues to evolve. Bon voyage, and until we meet again under the shadow of Fourvière, farewell from the captivating city of Lyon!

Printed in Great Britain
by Amazon